I
Jonathan, t

Brita Long, Attorney at Law PLLC

©2019 All rights reserved.

***

Contents

ABOUT THIS BOOK 1

INTRODUCTION 3

CHAPTER ONE: 9
The Tradition of Hourly Billing

CHAPTER TWO: 15
The Problems with Hourly Billing

CHAPTER THREE: 49
Why Flat Fees Are Amazing

CHAPTER FOUR: 55
How to Set Your Flat Fee

CHAPTER FIVE: 71
Communicating About Flat Fees to Others

CHAPTER SIX: 83
Essential Elements of Flat Fee Billing

CHAPTER SEVEN: 95
Handling Common Issues That Arise From Flat Fee Billing

CHAPTER EIGHT: 107
Time Management Tools of Successful Attorneys

CHAPTER NINE: 129
Is This Working?

CONCLUSION 133

ABOUT BRITA LONG 135

***

ABOUT THIS BOOK

The greatest threat to the integrity
of the legal system is a broke
and unhappy attorney.

Whether you are new to the practice or have been practicing law since the Ford Administration, you should be paid — in full — for the work you perform. You should be paid for your superior judgment, your skills, your ability to negotiate, and your knowledge — not how many hours you took to draft a pleading. *The Happier Attorney: A Comprehensive Guide to Charging Flat Fees for Legal Services* is a step-by-step guide that will teach you:

- What hourly billing is really costing you in money, and more importantly, time.

- Why hourly billing is bad for clients and horrible for attorneys.

- Why clients love flat fees.

- How you can obtain a collection rate of 100%.

- How flat fees improve your work product.

- How flat fees will increase your income significantly.

- How flat fees will save you so much time you won't know what to do with your time.

- How flat fees will decrease staff time and costs.

- How to manage your time so that you can meet your responsibilities and have lots of time outside the office.

- How to ethically and easily address any issues that arise from flat fee billing.

    In the nearly 19 years of owning her own practice, and well over a decade of using exclusively flat fees, even for family law litigation, Brita Long is in a unique position to share everything that you would want and need to know when you are considering moving from hourly billing to flat fees.

    The relief of only working as many hours as you want to work, and still make the money you want to make, and have earned, is only a few hours away.

* * *

INTRODUCTION

"Success is not the key to happiness.
Happiness is the key to success."

–Albert Schweitzer

As attorneys, we are overworked. No matter how much we work, there is pressure to work even more. This occurs regardless of whether our work product suffers as a result. The quality of our work product, whether it is effective or efficient, is secondary to the number of hours we bill.

This work load can lead to misery. We are miserable to ourselves and miserable to everyone else. We have every reason to be miserable. What we are doing isn't working. What we're actually doing is so farfetched that many good attorneys are leaving the profession. I believe that hourly billing is a large part of the problem and fixing how we charge for our services would go a long way to resolve the discontent in our profession.

Our legal culture's issues won't be addressed overnight. However, flat fee billing is a shift that will have a major impact and can be implemented almost immediately. The benefits of using flat fees are simple: Happier and more satisfied clients; a better work product; happier staff; more time; more money; and far less stress.

It's actually possible to be an attorney who loves what they do, makes great money, has good relationships with clients, and leaves the office at noon every Friday without ever working on the weekends. Seriously, it is totally doable. However, you need to shift your mindset that in order to be a "good" attorney or earn a healthy income, you must work 50, 60, or 80 hours a week.

I know flat fee billing works because I've used it for over a decade. I used to be just as miserable as other attorneys. I worked way too much. Sometimes, I'd get into the office at 5:30 a.m. and still wasn't making the money I thought I should be making. I was constantly holding my breath for the next client to hire me and worrying about who would pay what each month when my billing statements went out. I didn't like chasing after my clients to pay me or withdrawing from the case when they couldn't. I knew there had to be a better way.

I knew that taking time to fill out time sheets over the course of a day was a waste of time. I knew spending hours each month reviewing them, cutting time, sending them out, and then praying for checks to begin to come in was ridiculous. I knew there had to be a better way.

I began looking for that better way. I was fortunate enough to find another attorney who had also been searching for an alternate way of billing. I read a book about an attorney using flat fees. I started using flat fees based on his work. Over the years, I examined, tweaked, examined more and tweaked more until I made flat fees my own, and built a system that worked for me. This is that system.

As you read, I would simply ask that you listen for the sake of listening. As attorneys, we are trained to listen not for the sake of understanding or consideration, but with the purpose of tearing the facts or argument apart. Or alternatively, finding the facts or arguments that we agree with.

I am going to ask that you turn off your attorney brain for just a minute. I would ask that you read and simply listen for just a minute and leave any judgment aside. I am not here to convince you to use flat fees. I am here to give a roadmap to those who wish to consider an alternative way to charge for their legal services.

This way of charging for your services — or parts of it — may not fit you. That is fine. Use what works for you and discard or tweak the rest.

What is most important is that you find a way to charge for your services while getting back to what you loved about law in the first place. That you work a reasonable number of hours each week and when you are at work, you are actually being productive and getting stuff done. That you have a healthy relationship with your clients and not one of an adversary. That you are being paid for your knowledge, your judgment, your experience, and your value — not how many hours you spent drafting a pleading.

It truly is possible to be a happier attorney.

- Flat fee billing, or various elements discussed in the book, may not be ethically allowed in your state or your particular area of practice. Please review your state's RPCs as well as any applicable ethical comments or opinions before implementing. If there is a particular element that is not ethical in your state, there is generally a work around that you could use in order to still charge flat fees. If you are not able to implement flat fees at all, perhaps this book can serve as an opportunity to start a conversation with your state's Bar Association about the benefits of flat fees.

- Any names used in this book are fictitious, to protect confidentiality and privacy. Family Law and Estate Planning, Probate and Trust Administration are mentioned as examples, only as those were my areas of practice. Flat fees can be used in most areas of practice.

* * *

CHAPTER ONE:
The Tradition of Hourly Billing

"Tradition becomes our security, and when the mind is secure it is in decay."

–Jiddi Krishnamurti

I have been a practicing attorney for more than 21 years and in the legal profession for more than 25. I have yet to hear anyone espouse the virtues, or any pleasures, of hourly billing for legal services. In its simplest form, hourly billing is exchanging money for one's time while working on a legal matter. That can be in the form of an attorney's time, paralegal, legal assistant, or even document clerk. Generally, our time is divided into increments of 6 minutes, with a minimum of .2 (12 minutes) and time is rounded up. So, if we talk with a client on the phone for 15 minutes, we charges .3.

Hourly billing actually isn't that old. Attorneys used to use a minimum fee schedule, which meant that the Bar Association essentially set a price for a matter. Attorneys even faced disciplinary action if the fee schedule was not used. That was until 1975, when the United State Supreme Court struck down minimum fee schedules as a violation of federal anti-trust law. Goldfarb v. Virginia State Bar, 421 US 773 – Supreme Court 1975. A nice summary of the history of legal fees was written by Sean Braswell in the Daily Dose, September 20, 2015.

> *Throughout the 19th century, legal fees in the U.S. were largely capped by state law with the costs of litigation footed by the losing party. More adventuresome billing methods, including retainers and contingency fees, began to crop up in the early 20th century. But, as litigation, corporate transactions and other legal work grew more complicated and expensive, many lawyers found themselves working harder and longer for the same standardized fee and, perhaps more importantly, falling well behind the pay scales of fellow professionals such as doctors and dentists.*

The Goldfarb ruling thus paved the way for hourly billing. Some argue that hourly billing persists because it gives clients some basis for auditing how they are billed. While in theory that may be true, I contend that in practice, the majority of clients don't want to spend the time or money auditing their bill and the costs of hourly billing far outweigh the benefits.

As attorneys, it certainly appears that we simply have grasped at straws in regard to billing for our services rather than evaluating what method of billing will pay us fairly, is efficient, and is still fair for our client. It is not clear that hourly billing has ever worked well, other than for those attorneys who are highly proficient at running the meter. What is clear to many attorneys and clients is that what may have worked in the past doesn't necessarily work today.

So why don't we just change it and fast? Well along with the meter running attorneys who like it (although they are still not recognizing its costs), I would argue that we keep hourly billing largely because we don't like change.

Even though hourly billing is less than 50 years old, it is how most attorneys are used to billing. Even older attorneys have used this billing method for the majority of their career. People in general don't like change. We as attorneys loath it. Hell, I still know a few practicing attorneys who don't use email. Our entire gig is about keeping the "status quo" and relying on precedent. It takes quite a bit for us to change our mind.

We pride ourselves on being methodical, patient, and not being affected by momentary changes in the tide.

We as attorneys also have the issue that our entire identities are wrapped up in how many hours we bill each day. We are the epitome of the "glorification of busy." We attorneys like to think that we are logical beings and that we don't let our emotions make decisions for us.

It is nearly laugh-out-loud funny that we have tricked ourselves into thinking we are so logical when so many of our decisions are based on emotions. It turns out we do have emotions, just like every other human being. How many times do we casually brag to one another about how many hours we billed that year? How many times do we lament on how busy we are and that we are just so tired of working on Sundays? How often do we leave evidence for our colleagues to see that we worked late that night or all weekend? We have all done it. It is our badge of honor — the way we judge each other and ourselves. We rationalize it as "the law is a jealous mistress."

We are also scared. Yes, attorneys are scared. We are scared of change. We are scared of doing something many attorneys are not doing, and we are terrified of being criticized or mocked by other attorneys. Yes, there are the few attorneys who don't care and seem to relish in being the outsider, but most of us fall in line fairly quickly and easily. That is because most, if not all of us, have experienced what happens in our world when one doesn't. We are fairly horrible to each other. We are judgmental, callous, unsupportive, and downright mean at times. That is a book for another time, but overall, we are not terribly nice to those of us who have any independent thoughts.

Think about writing a book about changing our entire fee structure knowing attorneys will be evaluating it. Now that is freaking scary. I have walked on the wings of a plane that was flying over the Puget Sound, and this is still more frightening. However, it must be said, so I will be the one to say it.

The way we treat hourly fees reminds me of a fairly well-known story.

A young lady is making dinner. As she is preparing the pot roast, she cuts off the end of the pot roast before putting it in the roasting pan. Her friend asks her why she just cut off the end of the pot roast. She indignantly replies that that is how you are supposed to prepare it. To prove she was right, the young lady called her mother to confirm that one was to cut off the end of a pot roast before putting it in the pan. Her mother confirmed that that is was indeed what one does. That is how her mother taught her and her mother knew how to cook. Her mother's method was beyond reproach.

The young lady's curiosity was not put to rest. The next time she was with her grandmother the young lady asked her grandmother why one would cut off the end of the pot roast before putting it in the pan. Her grandmother replied, "Well I only had one pan and it wasn't big enough for the pot roast, so I had to cut off the end."

So, is hourly billing really the best practice for getting paid for our services, or are we just cutting off the end of the pot roast for no reason other than that is what we have done for nearly 50 years, because at one point it was thought to have been a good billing method?

* * *

CHAPTER TWO
The Problems with Hourly Billing

> "The less there is to justify a traditional custom, the harder it is to get rid of it."
>
> –Mark Twain, *The Adventures of Tom Sawyer*

What we are doing is not working. It is bad for our clients, bad for us, and is a large contributor to why we are fairly miserable.

Yes, we are fairly miserable. We don't need a study to tell us that overall, we are a pretty unhappy group of people. Are you happy? Are your colleagues happy? People who are happy don't act like we act towards one another. We have high drug and alcohol issues, in addition to depression, anxiety, and suicide in our profession. One of the contributors to our discontent is how many hours most of us work.

Glorification of busy

We have created a mindset with hourly billing that an attorney's worth is based now on how clever they are, whether they have any emotional intelligence, or whether they do a good job or not. Our worth is solely derived by how many hours we bill per year. If we have met our billable hourly requirement, we can continue to play. If not, then we are of no use. It doesn't matter if our work saved that client five-million dollars or saved that client's life. Our only worth is how much you have billed. I am exaggerating only slightly.

I rented space in a larger firm years ago. One of the founding partners of the firm, we shall call him Tim, was a good attorney, a rain maker, and one of the pillars of the firm. This guy had made the firm a shit ton of money over the years. One year, for a few months, Tim went through a really rough time. His home burned to the ground. Literally, burned to the ground, leaving him and his family with no personal possessions, other than his second home. Then his mom died. Let's just set aside the trauma and emotional issues for a minute – after all, we are attorneys. Do you have any idea how much time it would take to find other housing and start to buy possessions back in order to have any sort of routine life, after your home burns to the ground? Do you have any idea the time it takes to deal with a dying parent or the time it takes to take care of an estate?

Either of these is a full-time job. Put them together, and I'm not sure how Tim made it through each day. However, Tim was still at work on most days.

Less than three months after these events, the managing partner of this firm, Bob, who was the nicest attorney in the firm, made a comment to me about Tim not pulling his weight and not being in the office. I just looked at Bob with a mixture of disbelief and sadness.

This is the culture that we have created. Shame on us.

We have created a culture in which attorneys are simply task workers. Attorneys are treated as if they are machines capable of working non-stop. Now billable, hour requirements are up to 2,500 hours a year. At 24 hours per day for 365 days a year, the maximum hours available are 8,760, yet we are now expecting attorneys to bill — not work — over 25% of all hours available in the entire year. It would be laughable if it were not true.

Even machines break down if they are overworked. Well, we are not machines. We are not designed to only work, sleep, and eat. When we are overworked, we break down and we don't do great work. Do you really think we are doing great work on the 79th hour we have worked that week? Do you really think we are doing great work when we have just been chastised for not working enough?

I knew of a senior attorney, Karen, who made the comment to an associate, Jared, that it was expected that Jared work all weekend. This was especially true since Jared "had gotten a Sunday off two weeks ago." Do you really think Jared did his best work that Sunday?

Hourly billing also creates a culture where it assumes that people's only incentive to work is getting paid. The more we work, the more we get paid. However, pay is not the only incentive to work. Pay is important, but so is not being miserable at work, having pride in one's work, making an impact, and actually wanting to be at work.

Conflict of interest
Actual conflict of interest

Billing by the hour does, of course, create actual and perceived conflicts of interest with our clients. We're deceiving ourselves if we argue otherwise. Even if it is not a conscious decision, when you get paid more, for working longer on a project, you're going to work on the matter longer. Especially if you know the client will just pay the bill every month. Just think of how you work on anything. If you know that you have three hours for a project, it generally takes the full three hours or close to it to complete. However, if you only have two hours for that same project, somehow you get it done in two hours. This is with any project or task, not just legal work. It is just human nature.

Then there are those attorneys, who we all know, who are professionals at running the meter. They are the ones that when you get a Notice of Appearance, you tell your client to sit down and brace for a long and bumpy ride. What kills me is that we all know who they are and yet time after time they get away with it. The judges don't seem to care, the Bar doesn't care, and their clients don't seem to care.

I had one divorce case in which the attorney on the other side, Lewis, had an unlimited war chest to finance litigation and his client was out for blood. Lewis was one of the big guys in Seattle and for the most part had a solid reputation. I had a previous case with him in which he was totally reasonable, and we settled the case easily and without any conflict. Well that was before he had an unlimited war chest. Lewis scheduled eight or nine depositions and we had, if I recall correctly, six. It was extremely rare for me to have even one deposition in a case. Having six was unheard of. He didn't get any useful information from any of the depositions, yet he kept going. And why not? His client was paying his bill every month. We ended up going to trial, which is rare for me as I am pretty reasonable and pride myself on having client control. The first day things were going so well for us that my client asked me, "Shouldn't he be trying to settle?" We prevailed on nearly every issue at trial. The court even made findings of facts on the party's credibility, which is rare in my experience. Lewis wasn't even phased. His attitude seemed to be that he was going to pump every single dollar he could out of this case regardless of the consequences to the children involved or frankly, his client.

How did Lewis's actions hurt his client? Well there is the obvious financial hit that his client took in that the case should have been probably $25,000, and it ended up being well over $100,000. More importantly, he continued to throw gasoline on a fire. His actions caused harm to the relationship between two parents with young children, and their families. The children were put through a custody battle which caused a lot of unnecessary stress for them. There was never a valid issue in the case. The children even had police contact and CPS came to their school. Their teachers were deposed. All because their father was out for blood. Instead of shutting him down, his attorney let him add gas to the fire. All for money. A few years after the case ended, the husband wanted to get back together with my client. I literally laughed out loud.

Besides the bill, what really infuriates me about those attorneys is the totally unnecessary damage they do. Our clients get their cues on how to behave from us. We have all had that client we can't control. Those are the clients who need to be liberated to find another attorney. Life is just too short. However, most clients will behave as we guide them. Not just with our words, but with our demeanor. When they come to us with a "he did X and I want to call in the firing squad," as long as we are calm, cool, collected, and explain why that is not in their best interest, most get it. They might not be happy about it, but they get it and keep a lid on things.

Maybe you are a corporate attorney and your client has "unlimited" funds. You send a bill every month and get a big fat check in return. There is a price to everything, my friend. No one really has unlimited funds. When you are padding your bill, you are taking money away from someone else. You are violating trust with each billing entry. If that doesn't bother you, then maybe you shouldn't be an attorney.

Perceived conflict of interest

There is also the perception from clients that there is a conflict of interest. They don't know that it really did take two hours to write that letter. They don't know the saying, "I would have made it shorter, but I didn't have the time." Even if you cut your time, there is always going to be the perception that you could have done it faster.

By charging by the hour, we are actually getting paid to be inefficient and ineffective. What incentive, other than our own morals, do we have to solve a problem by picking up the phone and talking to the opposing counsel, when that would only get us .4 when we can write a letter, read their responsive letter, write our own reply, maybe file a motion, and have the entire issue billed at 10.3? Especially if that month has been a "bad" month and we can totally justify all of the work. Even if someone questioned it, which who but the client would, we can justify it. Again, this isn't always, or even most of the time, a conscious thought pattern. It is just human nature.

The hourly fee model also pays absolutely no attention to the actual work product. Two attorneys are getting paid the same amount for two entirely different quality work products. Yes, there are attorneys who have pride in their work and there are a lot of attorneys who don't.

Whether your work is of actual value to the client or not is secondary, if considered at all, to how much one has billed. Providing your client with amazing value is rarely even considered in evaluating how the case went. It is based strictly on what you billed or if you "prevailed" in a motion or trial. Not what value, if any, was really obtained for the client.

I once had a client, Susan, come in for me to review her estate plan. She had a Revocable Living Trust that had been drafted and executed by an attorney in a big firm. She paid a ton of money for it. That didn't bother me, as I would have charged a lot for the value I would provide to her, as well. However, when I reviewed the trust, it was clear that it would not have met her minor children's needs or what she said was important to her. What was most alarming was that the trust was not funded. Susan, who was pretty sophisticated and intelligent, had never heard the word, much less been given any instructions on how to fund it. Her entire trust, which was frankly the most important piece of her estate plan, was totally useless.

Susan was not happy, and I can't blame her. She hadn't paid money to the big firm for some arbitrary documents. She paid money to ensure that her children would be properly cared for financially from a trust. She got little to no value from the work for which she had paid the price of a new car.

Horrible for clients

Besides the conflict of interest issues, hourly billing is horrible for clients.

Clients have no idea what a matter is going to cost. Even sophisticated clients don't have any idea. What other product or service would one purchase with no idea what it was going to cost and no control over that cost? That would be absurd, yet that is what we ask — demand — of our clients. There is no way for our clients to budget or even accurately come up with the money to handle the matter. This is especially true in litigation. Yes, you can give the client some "generally it costs between X and Y," but "generally" there is a large gap between those numbers.

Even low attorney fees can pose an issue when one doesn't know the final cost. For instance, my father recently died, and we had to hire an attorney to handle his relatively small estate. There were no issues with the probate. The attorney knew all of the assets, knew the liabilities, and knew that there were no issues that would come up. She charged a low retainer and her billing rates were reasonable. However, I had to budget for my father's cremation, funeral expenses, and her fees. It was imperative that I have some idea what her final fees would be or I would end up paying them. After being pressed repeatedly, she finally gave me a number, but of course it was a guestimate. It would be months before I knew the final bill and I had no control over it. From a client perspective, this uncertainty only adds to a very stressful situation.

Clients also get a false sense of the cost when they pay the initial fee. I know you go over the fee agreement with them, but they still have the impression that the initial fee will last for some time. It's a normal impression for them to have. If I just paid someone $5,000, I wouldn't expect to get another bill the next month. Yet, as we all know, $5,000 can be used with one motion or less. When I used hourly fees, I would repeatedly tell a client during the initial consultation that the initial fee was going to go quickly and that they needed to immediately be looking for more funds. Regardless of how emphatically I explained that to clients, there was still a disconnect there and they were still surprised just how quickly an initial fee goes.

So, what happens when the initial fee runs out? We all know what happens, as it has happened to us and we have seen it many times with others. You start sending bills to the client. The client has sticker shock, but most of the time makes a payment. Generally, not for anything close to the balance, but a good faith payment. Then the client stops calling you to ask questions or fails to tell you relevant information because they don't want to get charged for the phone call. This can be disastrous for their case.

Then next month's bill comes in and the charges are of course far higher than the payment they just sent in last month, but they send in another one. This goes on until the balance is high enough that you start getting antsy. So, you talk to them about making a larger payment, case not over yet, blah blah blah. The client doesn't have any more money to send. The balance is too high for you to keep adding to it without fear of the client walking away. So, you threaten to withdraw or actually withdraw.

Now, the client is in the middle of a legal matter, has no attorney, but still owes their attorney thousands of dollars and now has to go and find money to hire a new attorney. How is that reasonable or good for the client?

Hourly billing produces unhappy clients who don't like to pay their bill. Again, even in my father's really small matter, I would continually get annoyed when the attorney would not answer a question in an email and would wonder, "Is she going to bill me for the three emails I sent to her asking her to answer the same question that she hasn't answered?" Billing and final cost was always in the back of my mind.

Think about how you feel when you buy an airline ticket. You see the price, make a decision based on the price, and are excited for your trip. Then you get to the airport and have to pay $30 for a bag fee if you want to have your clothing with you on this trip. Isn't that annoying? Just tell me the freaking price– don't nickel and dime me. It is psychologically easier to spend the money once up front, than having to pay time and time again — even in small amounts. I once had a family law client, Bill, who gave up a piece of valuable real property worth far in excess of any child support he would owe his ex-wife, just so that he wouldn't have to write a check to her for child support every month. He didn't care. He didn't want the irritation of paying her each month.

Then there is the issue of what happens when the client owes you money and you get a bad ruling. You think they want to continue to pay you? Of course not. Even when they get favorable rulings or great settlements, people don't want to continue to pay you. It is human nature. The incentive to pay is there when you want something you don't have, not after you get it. How many times has this happened to you? When you are first hired, you are amazing. A legal genius. Within 24 hours of the case ending, even if you "won," you were "fine." Within two weeks, your client thinks he could have totally represented himself. Do you think that client has much incentive to pay you?

No, they are not horrible people. They are just people. We all think this way every day. When you need or want something, you value it far more than after you get it.

Of course, we again have the issue of attorneys padding their bills, running the meter, or intentionally escalating a case or at the least not deescalating the case, in order to be able to bill more. I think this is the worst thing that happens to clients as a result of hourly billing. How often does it happen or with how many attorneys? God only knows as there is no real way to monitor it. Judges and the Bar seem to turn a blind eye or have no interest in knowing, much less doing anything about it, only when things get totally out of hand and clients start making complaints that the bar steps in. Even then, the facts must be pretty outrageous.

    I have only known of one attorney who got in serious trouble for overbilling, and that was only brought to light because she wasn't representing clients diligently. We will call her Barbara. I actually worked for her. I went to work for her as a receptionist when I was waiting for my bar results. Barbara had an amazing office that was a quarter of the floor of a high rise. I knew nothing of caseloads, but I knew that her open case files took up an entire wall. I knew that there was no way one attorney could handle so many cases. I also answered the phones. I would get one or two phone calls a day from extremely angry clients who had not had their phone calls returned or had no idea what was happening in their matter.

    I knew when she came in each morning and knew that she generally didn't work on the weekends.

I also knew what she billed per hour. The math didn't work. And that was without me knowing what she paid in rent, which had to have been exorbitant. Barbara's husband worked for her, and I just assumed that he had family money or some other source of income that I didn't know about. They owned a nice home on an island and an antique yacht. I knew all of that was not coming from what she was making at the firm. There was also some talk about her client having sued her in a class action suit.

I wasn't even an attorney yet and I had no idea what was "normal," what rent and other office expenses were, or what a "normal" case load was. I also didn't know that it was rare for one client to sue you, much less a class action suit. Even with all of that ignorance, I knew that something was terribly wrong. There were a ton of really unhappy clients and that wasn't normal.

Barbara had teased me with "maybe we will hire you." I was a single mom with a large student loan debt and I needed a job. However, an actual offer never appeared. So, I looked elsewhere upon passing the bar and got another job. Thank goodness.

Sure enough a few years later, I was called into an interview with the Bar Association disciplinary investigator for a long interview about Barbara's practice. As it turned out, things were far worse than I could have imagined. Not doing the work she had been hired to do was the least of the issues. She had already gotten in trouble with the bar over her billing practices and lack of proper billing procedures. Yet she didn't change those practices or procedures for years. To say she over-billed is an understatement. She would bill for telephone conversations that didn't take place. She didn't keep itemized bills and refused to give client's explanations with regard to their bills. She billed .8 to file a Notice of Withdrawal. She was using her own rate when billing for legal assistance work. What is sad is that she was a good attorney, she just let greed get the better of her. She hurt her clients and not just by stealing from them.

Barbara's license to practice was suspended and she appealed the suspension. The WA Supreme Court agreed that her suspension was appropriate – and disbarred her.

Barbara is an extreme example and flew way too close to the sun — brazenly. How many other attorneys are doing the same thing, just to a smaller degree?

Bad for Attorneys

Morale

It's bad for morale when our focus is primarily on how much we bill.

Having a mandatory billing requirement is counterproductive. Even if one wanted to stay with hourly billing, having a mandatory billing requirement does the exact opposite of its intended purpose. I know it sounds crazy. "We need a mandatory billing requirement or attorneys won't bill enough and we won't make enough money." Wrong.

When I began writing my first book, my publisher instructed me that my writing requirement was 250 words per day. That was it. If I chose to exceed that writing requirement that was fine, but 250 words was completely acceptable. This requirement is ridiculously low in that 250 words is a few paragraphs. It would take years to finish writing a book with such a low bar every day. This requirement is set knowing full well that there is no way one can only write 250 words. Even on my worse writing day, when I would rather clean my baseboards, or anyone else's, one just can't write 250 words. The least that I have ever written in a day is over 850. Nearly four times my requirement.

Every word over 250 is a delight. It is a choice. I can stop at any time . . . but I don't.

Likewise, I recently heard of a Fortune 500 company that paid a very handsome sum to a consultant in the hopes of increasing sales. This company had a sales force, that according to management, was just not selling enough. After some inquiry and study, the consultant reached his conclusion: cut the sales teams goals by 90%. The company's management thought this guy was an idiot and they had just wasted a lot of money. Thankfully for them, they went ahead and tried it. Sure enough, sales increased. Now this is a totally anecdotal story, of which I cannot verify, however, it does ring true with my own experience.

Say nothing of the fact that mandatory billing requirements just keep increasing to absurd levels. When I became an attorney, even the worst big firms were at about 2,000 billing hours per year. Now they are up to 2,500. That is crazy. That means that one is in the office at least 12-14 hours per day. And you are supposed to be involved in the community, Bar Associations, and doing pro bono as well. Sleep? Sleep is for the weak, my friend. When exactly is someone supposed to eat, shower, get ready for work, get to and from work, sleep even a minimal amount of time, and work 14 hours per day for 5, 6, or even 7 days a week? Not to mention having any sort of enjoyment in life. And for the big prize of what? Doing it for five years plus to *maybe* get a shot at being a partner? And the big prize of being partner is? More money and prestige. Not working much less.

Am I the only person who looks at this game with a "what the f. .ck" look on my face? I have never gotten it. Before law school, I worked at a large law firm in Phoenix. The surface trappings were lovely shiny balls. Beautiful office, prestige, having to wear fancy clothing, and walk by large corner offices of the attorneys who "had made it." It didn't take long before the shine had worn off. Yes, the senior partner drove a new Jaguar. He drove it home to his third wife. I saw associates crying as they walked down the hallway in the middle of the day — so done with trying to keep it together that they didn't even make it to the bathroom to cry.

I have known enough people in large firms that I know these stories are not unique. I had a friend, Carrie, who went to the bathroom once during the day. During her restroom time a client emailed her. Carrie's supervising partner happened to be on vacation, although she was still billing eight hours a day. By the time Carrie returned to her office her supervising partner, Mary, had answered the client's email and had emailed Carrie chastising her for not replying to the client's email in a timely manner. Not kidding.

Was this managing partner a happy person? Of course not. NO one who is happy acts like that. This partner, Mary, was a great attorney and highly respected. She worked non-stop. She had no interests, no friends, no kids, and died of a brain tumor at age 64. Even her obituary read mostly of how much she worked. At the end of the day, what was her purpose? What impact did Mary make in the world? If all anyone can say about you when you die is that you worked hard . . . well that is sad.

The psychological stress of hourly billing is always present. If one has integrity, one is constantly thinking about that conflict in each time entry made. Is it too much? It really did take that long, but how will I explain that to my client? This client isn't paying me and won't, yet here I am waiting to argue a motion to get their money. Do you really think you are doing great work at that point? Are you really focused on giving it your all or just going through the motions? Or are you thinking about how you can get any money received to pass through your office so that you can get your fees paid?

When clients don't pay or are slow to pay, it does affect how you feel about them. I consider myself to be a fairly generous person, probably more generous than most. I enjoy giving to people, but I don't like someone taking from me. To me, a client not paying their bill, absent extreme circumstances, is stealing. It is no different than going into my purse and taking out money. It leaves a bad taste in your mouth. Then you're far less trusting of the next poor soul who walks into your office. How are they going to pay for this? How can you ensure that they pay for all of your services?

You start an adversarial relationship with your client from the get-go even if you don't mean to because you have been burned so many times.

There have also been times when my pride has been hurt when clients haven't paid their bill. I take a lot of pride in my work. I took on cases that other attorneys wouldn't. I have tenacity and would not give up on the hard cases. We put our entire lives into cases, especially litigation and family law litigation. To go through what we go through and then turn around to have our clients not pay us, is disheartening to say the least.

So, how do you try to remedy these problems? You try to change your fee agreement, write amazing descriptions, get bills out the same day every month, you are "on it" when clients are late, you even try the evergreen trust account method . . . and still don't get paid what you are owed. Yet, the bills remain, your rent still needs to get paid and your staff expects a check every two weeks.

Maybe you are one of the attorneys who are earning a lot of money. That is great. I would mention that there are a lot of attorneys who are not making a lot of money, and some are just barely getting by – really. I would suggest that you could make even more money if you were not billing by the hour. I will show you how in the next chapter.

While you may be billing and even collecting a lot, hourly billing costs you a lot to administer. Forget the time for a second. The cost you are paying for staff to put bills put together, send them out, handle payments, and manage bookkeeping, adds up every month. The vast majority of this is wasted money. Why pay your staff for doing a job that really isn't necessary, when you could be paying to work on projects that will bring in more clients? Maybe you don't need as much staff at all?

For attorneys who don't have a full case load and are not collecting all their fees from their clients, it can be really difficult to budget as they really don't know how much money will be in their accounts each month. I remember those days. "Well if X client pays at least Y, then I can pay these bills." It was really challenging. With flat fees, you know from the get-go what you have to spend, as even one or two clients will get you enough funds to be able to budget for the month, depending on your costs of course. However, it is far easier to budget knowing you have $20,000 to work with rather than $5,000 and the hope of another $15,000 coming in that month.

With hourly fees, you are not paid in full for your work. Most attorneys, the honest ones, actually don't bill their clients for all of the time they worked on a matter. Then on top of that, they cut their time before the bills go out.

By the way, if you are billing for your staff and cutting their time, they probably don't appreciate it. You are sending them the message that their time is not valuable. I remember when I was a document clerk, I was to track my time, write great descriptions for making yet another set of copies, only to have the managing partner, Jan, cut all of my time. I was told she just didn't believe that the client should be billed for a document clerk's work. Okay, fine. Then why have me keep track of my time? It was a bit disheartening. I had pride in my work. I was helping the firm make money. I was bringing in X dollars to the firm each month. Oh, no I wasn't since she just cut my time to zero.

So, you are already not getting paid for your work. Then your client either doesn't pay or doesn't pay all of the bill. Even with the best screening and systems, you are going to get clients who don't pay their bill. One bad client can do some big damage. If you are solo and a client walks on a $8,000 bill, that hurts. Have one or two of those a year, along with other clients who don't pay their bills, and it really adds up. Even if your collection rate is relatively high, say 85%, you are still losing anywhere from $45,000 - $150,000, or more, depending on your hourly rate and billed hours. What difference in your life could that money make?

Again, this creates mistrust and resentment towards your clients in general. Your staff feels the same way, in that they have worked hard for the clients as well, and yet that client doesn't value the work enough to pay for it.

Hourly billing also creates stress for staff because they can't tell if the firm is financially sound or not. However, they hear the rumblings and feel your stress over finances. Think this is just with small firms? Nope. I have enough friends in large firms to know it is not. I had one friend who was on the finance committee in a large firm who wondered if her paycheck was going to bounce, given the firm's financial situation. When I first moved to Seattle, a large firm had just imploded and sent shock waves throughout the state. It turned out that each partner was carrying over $250,000 of debt for the firm, and that was in the late 1990s. That is astonishing.

Flat fee billing will not magically solve all financial woes. It does however provide far more certainty than hourly billing.

Evergreen account

What about an evergreen trust account policy? That is when a client pays X upfront and it is put in a trust account. There must be a minimum in the trust account at all times. For instance, the client pays $10,000 and when there is only $2,500 remaining in the trust account for that client, the client must pay another X amount to cover future fees. In theory, you will always be paid for your work as you will always have $2,500 in your trust account for the client.

What sounds great on paper, in my experience, didn't work well and was a pain in the rear. First of all, I am not an accountant. In college, I received a low C and a D in the two accounting classes I took. When I first started my own practice, I did my own books and somehow managed to get through it. However, it wasn't long before I hired an accountant/bookkeeper to handle the office finances and books. When using an Evergreen account, you are going in and out of your IOLTA a lot. The more you go in and out, the higher the chances are of a mistake being made. As you well know, mistakes regarding an IOLTA account are not acceptable in any way, shape, or form and must be reported to the bar association. That is not a conversation I ever want to have.

Secondly, whether it's you or a bookkeeper, it involves a lot of work and will take a lot of time. Time that you are either not making money or are paying someone else to do that work. And that is if everything goes as planned.

In my experience, it was difficult to monitor each client's account in real time to see when they were getting close to the minimum amount. Even when the client did, we were generally in the middle of storms and we couldn't stop work. So, we blew past the minimum every single time. Maybe someone else has a great way of monitoring it or doing it, but it didn't work for me at all.

Time

One of the largest problems with hourly billing is that it is a total waste of time. Time is the most precious resource any of us have. We all get the same 24 hours a day. When we calculates how much time we are truly spending on entering time, reviewing bills, answering client's questions or concerns, trying to collect from clients, and dealing with the bookkeeping, it is really surprising. The numbers don't lie. So, let's look at them.

For at least a week, preferably a few, keep a notepad by you and time how long it takes you every day just to enter your time. Then track for a few months how much time you are spending on all issues related to billing. Also, have your staff track their time on all billing related tasks.

What are the numbers? For most attorneys, even the really organized ones, the numbers are surprising. Most average over 140 - 180 hours per year just on the administration of hourly billing. The average is over 20 work days per year of completely wasted time. And that is just for the attorney. That isn't counting what you are paying staff. On top of the actual time spent on entering time, you are constantly interrupting your thought process to enter the time. "They" say that it takes the brain 10- 23 minutes to regain full focus after each interruption. Well if you are keeping contemporaneous notes, you are interrupting your brain continually throughout the day.

Let's look at your numbers.

- How many hours are you using each week to track time? Multiply that by 47 weeks. _____

    (I am using 47 for illustration purposes, assuming when adding up time, you are not billing for at least four weeks.)

- How many hours average per month is spent reviewing bills, talking with clients about bills, any collection efforts, or any other time spent on billing? _____

- What is the amount of time you are spending on hourly billing each year? _____

- What could you be using that time for instead? Maybe seeing your family, spending time doing something you enjoy, or working on getting more clients in the door?

The financial costs of hourly billing

There are also the actual financial costs of using an hourly billing method.

Again, for a month or two, calculate the following:

- How much time do you cut off of bills each month? _____

- How much staff time is used for billing matters? Sending out, getting in mail or phone, bookkeeping, etc.? _____

- Multiply their pay rate by the hours. What is the actual cost? _____

- What is your collection rate? What did you bill last year vs. what you were actually paid for? _____

- What is this hourly rate actually costing you financially? _____

- How could this money better serve your life?

Feelings

"Oh, crap she is going to talk about feelings." I know we are attorneys and we don't bother with trivial things like feelings. Even the word makes us very uncomfortable. We are above feelings. Whatever people. Is that why we have a lot of attorneys who have significant drug and alcohol issues? Or why they're having affairs and other self-destructive behaviors? Who in our profession doesn't have an anxiety disorder, anger issue, or depression issue? How do I know we are not dealing well with our feelings? Again, look at the way we treat one another. We are fairly vicious to each other. We justify our behavior by "I'm just advocating for my client," when in reality no one who is happy acts like that.

Please name five, okay one, attorney you know who loves their job. I mean, can't wait to get in the office every morning, whistling through the halls, smiling at everyone they meet, happy.

Of course, I am not suggesting that flat fees will cure all of the happiness issues with attorneys. I do contend that much of the stress that we have as attorneys is due to hourly billing and the unrealistic pressure that we impose on ourselves to make money. I would also contend that hourly billing does grate away at our pride in working hard for a client only to have that work not valued. I would also contend that we do not do our best work when we are unhappy, and we are unhappy a lot of the time.

Just think of what kind of work you could produce if you had the following life:

- Worked a maximum of 35-40 hours per week. If you wanted to work more you could, but you didn't have to.

- Your work was valued and you were paid for your work in full.

- You had a healthy relationship with your clients and money was never thought about or discussed after being hired. Your full concentration was on the work product and only the work product.

- You were making double or triple the income you are currently making.

Do you think your work would be the same? Better? It certainly wouldn't be worse right?

So, let's think about how you really feel about hourly billing. I know filling this out may seem silly, but bear with me. It is one thing to think something in your head and another matter to see in in black and white. No one is going to see this, so please just do it and be honest. This is here to help you.

How many hours did you bill last year? _____

Name a time when a client questioned their bill? _____

Have you ever done a different quality of work or put in different effort in a case based on if you thought they would pay? _____

Name some opposing counsel you know who have a reputation for creating conflict in cases so that they can collect additional fees. _____

How do you feel when that opposing counsel is on the other side of the case? _____
_____
_____
_____

Name a case where you did amazing work for your client only to have that client turn around and not pay you. _____

How did that make you feel? _____
_____
_____
_____
_____

So now that you have some numbers on how much time and money is being wasted, how does that feel to you? _____
_____
_____
_____
_____

If you feel something is off, amiss, or that there has got to be a better way of getting paid for our legal services, then keep reading.

* * *

CHAPTER THREE
Why Flat Fees Are Amazing

"Simplicity is the ultimate form of sophistication."

Leonardo de Vinci

Flat fee billing is the simplest form of exchanging legal services for money. It is having a set price for a set matter, with a specific ending event or time. Nothing more and nothing less. Just like how you purchase everything else in your life. I contend that it is a superior way of charging for our services for the client, for the attorney, and for the legal community, while producing a higher quality of work.

The benefits of flat fee billing are the antithesis of the problems with hourly billing. The benefits for clients are that they know what a matter is going to cost and can make an informed decision on whether to proceed. The client can budget for the legal matter. The client doesn't have anxiety about their bill, as there is no further bill. The client isn't hesitant to talk to the attorney and ask questions.

In my experience, other benefits have emerged that one would not necessarily think about. Clients are far more cooperative. Clients appreciate you far more and value your work. There is a psychological effect of paying a larger fee, especially in one or two payments. The clients have more skin in the game than with hourly billing and don't have to spend time or energy constantly worrying about finding more money or writing more checks every month. If a client has an attorney, regardless of the case or matter, they have enough to worry about. They want to write one or two checks and be done with it. Clients absolutely love flat fees.

Since I have been charging flat fees, I have not had one client or prospective client want to be charged an hourly rate or even ask about it. Clients totally get it and appreciate the simplicity.

Staff like flat fees far better than hourly billing methods. First, their time is not wasted in having to deal with all of the billing issues. They are not dealing with angry clients calling about their bills. Remember, they are on the front lines and get the brunt from angry clients. They know that the firm's finances are in good shape and don't need to worry about who will pay what this month either. The morale in the office is far better overall as the attorneys are happier. Happier attorneys are nicer to staff. Overall the firm culture and morale are improved. An emphasis is on efficiency, effectiveness and doing a great job for the client.

Flat fees are great for attorneys. I know that I felt relief the day I switched to flat fees. I didn't have to constantly think about the money. I could just work on the case. I could concentrate far better and my work product improved. I had always considered myself to be a very ethical attorney. I have never padded my bills – quite the opposite. I hadn't really realized though how much I had thought about whether someone was going to pay me or not and how that affected my work product until I switched to flat fees. I realized that in past cases, I didn't give it my all as I was afraid I wouldn't get paid. I am not just talking about how much time I spent doing something, but deeper than that. With flat fees I was totally free. My strategies became laser focused, I took a bigger picture approach to cases, and it felt like I was really solving problems, not just going through the motions. I enjoyed my work more. I was producing work that I was really proud of.

I had the incentive to get it done. Get it done quickly and well. I guess it comes down to focus. I could focus more with flat fees — and I did. Any subconscious bias towards clients was gone. I was rewarded for being efficient and effective. I was rewarded for thinking of a solution that saved my client money, time, and grief. I was paid for giving value to my clients. There was less anxiety with cases and people. Not just about the money, but overall. It didn't matter if the other side was being a pain, it wasn't hurting my client anymore financially. One would think that that would bother you with flat fees, as then you are doing more work for the same money, but it doesn't. "You aren't running up my client's fees. File away." This new attitude changed the dynamics of the case, and I really think opposing counsel backed off a bit. It was just a totally different mindset. One that I can't fully explain. One just has to experience it for themselves.

I liked my clients more. I didn't have any underlying thoughts of whether I could trust them to pay me or not. I didn't have fear of not being able to pay the bills and could plan accordingly. No longer would a client ever take from me.

I wasn't wasting my time. My staff wasn't wasting their time. I wasn't trapped in cases anymore or chasing clients for money. It just wasn't an issue. I had far more time, more money, was a kinder person, had far less anxiety and was just a happier attorney. I just didn't have the hassles and stress of hourly billing.

I even made more money when I went to flat fees. And not just because I was collecting all of my fees, which increased my income as well as reduced administration costs. Even taking all of that into account, I just made more money. For those who have billing requirements of 2000 – 2500 hours per year, I am here to tell you that you can bring in the same money and work 40-50 hours per week. I am totally serious and I will show you how.

Let's say you bill 2,000 hours per year and your hourly rate is $450 per hour. You have 10 new matters per month on average. The maximum that you can ever bring in is $900,000. And that assumes a 100% collection rate. With flat fees, even with the same 10 new matters each month you charge the average flat fee for each matter is $12,000. Your new gross income with flat fees is $1,440,000. You are also working far less in that you don't have the administration time and you are working far more efficiently.

Deep down, I think we all know that simple is better than complex. So, I hope that I have piqued your interest enough to at least try using flat fee billing. As with everything else, the devil is in the details, and implementing flat fees properly is the key to having a successful transition.

* * *

CHAPTER FOUR
How to Set Your Flat Fee

"Simplicity is complexity resolved."

Brancusi

As attorneys we tend to overcomplicate matters. We are trained to find the "what ifs" and sometimes we even manufacture them. Please be vigilant about keeping this process as simple as possible. To not be tempted to overcomplicate it in any way. This is not rocket science and you will need to make adjustments as you go along. We are used to being "right" and not having all of the answers right away, much less having to adjust as you go along, may be uncomfortable to you. Get over it and keep going.

In order to implement flat fees, you will have to complete your foundational research. What is this foundational research? Simply put: it is what you are normally charging your clients for the work performed. "But all cases are different," you say. Yes and no. Generally, regardless of the practice area, even with litigation, you can break cases into a few categories.

For instance, in family law, one might classify cases into:

Easier than expected: normal people, not contentious, doing some math and for the most part reasonable people and working toward an easy resolution. The case where you tell your client that he and his soon to be ex-spouse should write a book on how to get divorced and keep your wits and dignity.

Normal case: spouses blaming each other for the divorce, the other isn't a good parent, need to get temporary orders, maybe a temporary restraining order, or drug/alcohol issues, send and receive a few nasty letters back and forth to opposing counsel, maybe a GAL is involved, but ultimately you know it will settle in mediation or a settlement conference – and it does. These are the ones where you hope everyone gets into therapy and you are just glad it is done.

The holy shit case: These are the cases you get once every 3-10 years that make you seriously consider giving up the practice of law all together.

In Estate planning one might have:

Simple Individual Will and auxiliary documents.

Simple Married couple wills and ancillary documents.

Revocable Living Trust

> RLT with

> RLT with

With funding or without.

Whatever your practice area, you can categorize your matters into certain groups. Again, don't overcomplicate this process. We are just trying to get some baseline categories to begin working with. You can tweak them later on if needed.

Once you have your categories, let's look at what you have changed for matters in that category, and then average them out. You may be very surprised. Again, don't overcomplicate this process. Just pick a random sampling of 5-10 matters in each category, add up their total fees, and then average them out.

Are you surprised at the numbers? I remember when I first began researching for flat fees, I was shocked when I looked at the final numbers for cases. I remember one in particular was a family law case that was a normal case. My client was low maintenance, but there was a history of domestic violence and we had a few hearings, but no trial. If you had asked me what I think the total was for her fees, I would have said maybe $15,000, but no more than $20,000. WRONG. Her total fees were over $31,000. When I kept doing the math, I realized that my perception of my fees was totally off and if I had just picked a number in my head without doing the research first, my flat fee would have been less than one-half of what it should have been.

Doing the research also is critical to being able to justify your flat fee to clients or anyone else. So do the research and keep it. I know it is a pain in the rear. Do it anyway.

What to charge?

This is an art, not a science. As much as I hate to ask you to do it, we are going to look at the Model Rules of Professional Conduct to begin. Every state of course has different rules, so please look at your specific state's RPCs in regard to fees. For our purposes, we will use the ABA model rules as a guide.

ABA Model rules

Rule 1.5: Fees

Client-Lawyer Relationship

(a) A lawyer shall not make an agreement for, charge, or collect an unreasonable fee or an unreasonable amount for expenses. The factors to be considered in determining the reasonableness of a fee include the following:

(1) the time and labor required, the novelty and difficulty of the questions involved, and the skill requisite to perform the legal service properly;

Clearly the problem with this element is that if something only took you an hour, it is because you just spent the last twenty years learning how to do it well in an hour. It does however work into flat fees in that you are charging for your skills. So, ==if you are highly skilled in one area, then charge for that skill.==

(2) the likelihood, if apparent to the client, that the acceptance of the particular employment will preclude other employment by the lawyer;

Of course, accepting a particular matter will preclude you from other employment. You can only take on so many matters and you can't take on any matter in which there will be a conflict of interest. This particular element doesn't seem terribly relevant to the issue of how much to charge for your flat fee.

(3) the fee customarily charged in the locality for similar legal services;

I really dislike this rule, but it is what it is. First of all, price fixing was ruled to be illegal, so I am not sure why this element is still around. In any event, this is where your research comes in handy if anyone questions your flat fee.

(4) the amount involved and the results obtained;

Here is where flat fees shine. You are getting paid for the value you are providing to your client. If my quick thinking just saved a client $1 million, then I should be compensated accordingly. To say that I should only be compensated for that .5 it took to come up with that solution is ridiculous. Again, it took 20 years of experience, several books, countless seminars, and hours of learning to come up with that solution.

(5) the time limitations imposed by the client or by the circumstances;

This is also a key provision for flat fees. When I charged by the hour, there was absolutely no difference between what I got paid for normal work and what I got paid for "holy crap, this needs to get done now work." How many times did a client come in with an emergency and I needed to file a well-written pleading in less than 48 hours? I remember one incident in which my client dropped off photos of his children with hand print bruises on a Friday afternoon. I worked that weekend, on Easter Sunday, and had an Ex Parte

Motion for Restraints signed and filed that Monday morning. Later the Judge questioned the timing of the motion and asked when I received the photographs. I told him Friday afternoon. He then questioned when I drafted the pleadings. I looked him dead in the eye and said, "Sunday. Easter Sunday." He asked no further questions.

I had another client who was literally on her death bed when we did her estate plan, including a family trust. We were able to draft her estate plan, have it executed, and fund the trust, in less 72 hours. Everything else in the office came to a dead halt. It was every man on deck. That is flipping extraordinary and not how I like to work, but we did it. You bet we should be compensated for that in excess of what we would normally charge.

==Most of the time client "emergencies" are at least due in part to their own behavior. So yes, I am going to charge more for having to work in high gear.== This is easy with flat fees. One just adds on an additional expedited fee.

(6) the nature and length of the professional relationship with the client.

This is not terribly applicable to the question of what to set your flat fees to.

(7) the experience, reputation, and ability of the lawyer or lawyers performing the services; and

This is another element in which we can shine with flat fees. If you need brain surgery, who do you want to perform the surgery? I want the best freaking surgeon in the entire world and if I have the money, I would pay them whatever they wanted for a fee. What are their services worth? A lot more than a difference of $100 or even $500 an hour, that's for sure.

So, if you have extraordinary experience, a solid reputation, and have a special ability that others don't have, you should be compensated for that as you are providing extra value to the client.

(8) whether the fee is fixed or contingent.

This isn't terribly relevant to the issue of setting flat fees.

So when starting to set your fees, make sure you review your state's RPCs in regard to fees. I also recommend starting with a checklist of the different factors when setting your fee. This will of course depend on your practice area.

Such as:

Type of case or matter: easy, normal, or holy crap. What is your baseline for each based on your average? Are there children involved?

Client: Easy client who is going to listen and do what you suggest or high maintenance client who you are going to have to spend more time with? Obviously, you charge more for a difficult client.

Opposing party: Who is the opposing party? Are they a fighter? Do they have a drug or alcohol problem? Do they have funds to continue on a prolonged fight? Is there domestic violence? Do they have a personality disorder?

Opposing counsel: Who is on the other side? Is it someone who is reasonable or someone who is going to throw gas on the fire and increase fees? Is the attorney competent or are you going to have to draft every pleading and order to ensure it is correct?

Funds: What funds are involved? What value are you going to provide your client?

You should have a fairly set price range for matters before a client walks in the door, and then you set the price according to the client and their needs. I will give you a few examples.

Family law

Let's say your baseline for a "normal" case is $30,000. You read your client's questionnaire before they come in the door and see that attorney "ex parte guy" is on the other side. Fee just went up by at least

$3,000-5,000. You meet with your client and they seem reasonable, is able to take responsibility for their actions, isn't blaming everything on their ex, and wants to settle matters reasonably. When you tell them what to do, they immediately nod their head and don't fight you. Their soon-to-be ex has an alcohol issue though. That means that they probably aren't going to be so reasonable, especially given that their attorney will add fuel to the fire. That adds on another few thousand. The parties don't have much in the way of assets, so the finances aren't that much of a consideration for setting your fee.

So, at the end of the consultation you tell the client the flat fee, not including trial, will be $37,000. That is it.

Now let's say that you have some special expertise in dealing with addicts. That is highly valuable to your client. Charge for that expertise. Add on another $3,000 or whatever.

Where a GAL is Necessary

Estate planning

I had a set range for Wills and Trusts depending on what type of trust and if we were funding the trust or not. I also had a higher set of fees for estates valued in excess of $3,000,000. I even had the price sheet laminated so that my clients knew the prices were static.

Adjust your fees

Every single year, let's just pick January, at least consider adjusting your set fees upward. Your costs are going up every year and your income should as well. I know it can be uncomfortable. Do it anyway.

"But I am brand new and don't have any history on which to base my fee."

Well then you are going to just have to guess the first few times and track your time to see if you are in the right ball park. So, based on the last family law example, I might start out at $15K and my add ons would not be as high. You can always adjust the fee for the next client. Also, we will discuss further on downwardly adjusting a fee.

Reasonable

Regardless of what you charge, it must be "reasonable"— whatever that means. If you do a great job, you want your fees high. You want to be one of the highest paid attorneys in town and you will provide the value to justify that price. What is "reasonable"? I don't know. I think that it is fairly easy to spot an "unreasonable" fee, especially if it can't be supported. For instance, for an easy family law case, if your fee was $30K, that might be getting a bit high. If it was

$150K, then I don't know how you would justify that fee.

Now if your client was Jeff Bezos, then yes, a fee of $150K or even much higher could be completely justified given the amount of funds involved. So, can you justify your fee?

How to start

1. Do your research and have some idea of your basic fees and the other factors that will affect the fee.

2. Draft your fee agreement and know it inside and out — especially the provisions that are key to flat fees. We will address the fee agreement in a bit.

3. Train your staff. They are going to have to know how to communicate with prospective clients about flat fees, as well as changing the administration procedures. They will probably be pleased to not have to waste their time with hourly billing.

4. Make a cheat sheet for you to have for initials when you first begin quoting flat fees until you get the hang of it and can do it on your own.

5. Jump. The next prospective client that comes in, go through the initial, quote a number, and shut up. Don't be too eager to feel the need to defend the number. We will address sticker shock in a bit.

I was so nervous, but excited, when my first client sat down after I had decided to use flat fees. I had my justifications ready to go and I was ready to defend my price. At the end of the consultation, I quoted a number and it was a high number. A number that nearly stuck in my throat. The client didn't flinch. They paid the price and we got going. It was wonderful and I was hooked.

Another case came my way in which my client, Violet, had an uncle who was an attorney and a bigwig attorney at that. At first, I thought we may have an issue as he wanted to talk with me about my fees. The case didn't involve any money but had DV issues, maybe a personality disorder on the other side, and ex parte restraining orders. I knew that if Violet did what I told her to do, I could probably get her daughter back for her. What is the value for that? High. That is what it is. The case was also in another county, and I would have to drive at least two hours each way for hearings. I, however, was very familiar with that county, knew the judges and attorneys, and knew what I needed to do to stand a great chance of getting Violet's daughter back to her. Violet was a mess, but seemed malleable and ready to do what I told her to do. I will say though that given some of the facts, many other family law attorneys would have told her she didn't stand a chance of getting custody, she needed to just settle the case, and hope she got one-third time with her daughter.

I am not that attorney. I saw that with a lot of work and skill, we could walk that tightrope and there was a good chance of getting her daughter back.

I quoted her a fee of I think $20,000. Her uncle immediately paid the fee and wanted to talk with me. Again, I was ready to defend my fee and also remind him that he was not to interfere in the case, etc. What he wanted to tell me is that his niece might need a bit more hand holding that I had anticipated. Therefore, the fee needed to be increased by $10,000. Okay, I said.

He was correct. Violet did need a bit more handholding. However, she did what I told her to do, I was able to do a great job for her, and I will never forget her driving to go pick up her daughter when we obtained an order returning her daughter to her care and custody. I did a great job for Violet, she has her daughter to this day and is by far the better parent, and I was paid well for my services. Her uncle and I are still in touch.

In another family law case, a client, Sally, came in for an initial on a case that had already been filed. She was not happy with her current attorney. She was very anxious, nothing was her fault, and she knew what I needed to do. Guess what: the more she talked the more my fee kept jumping up and up. Sally was going to be beyond high maintenance, difficult to wrangle, and a pain in the rear. I would handle the case, but she was going to pay for the extra demands that would be present in this case. And not by a few thousand dollars extra either. I think I quoted an extra $10,000 above what I normally would have charged. And based on what I know now, I should have charged an extra $20,000 – not kidding.

So, remember that when you first set your flat fee, it is going to be an educated guess that you will need to monitor and adjust periodically for a bit. Once you get the hang of it, adjust on a yearly basis. Remember this is not science and be a bit flexible at the start. Above all, keep it simple. If for no other reason, you want to be able to explain your system to others.

***

CHAPTER FIVE
Communicating About Flat Fees to Others

"If you can't explain it simply, you don't understand it well enough."

Albert Einstein

One of the keys to making this new way of charging for your services successful is having clear communication about what this new method is. Remember, it is just the same as going into a store and buying a gallon of milk and paying a set price for said gallon of milk.

In discussing communication, I will start with what for most clients is their first or second contact with us, and that is our website. However, in all of your communication about flat fees, you should be reinforcing the benefits to the client of value pricing.

Flat Fee = Value Pricing

The value of Flat fee billing

==They will know the price for the matter before they ever agree to hire you. There will not be surprises in regard to your bill. They will never be left without an attorney. You will do a more efficient and effective job, as neither of you has to worry about future payments.==

I also trust that you can communicate the virtues of value pricing without denigrating other attorneys who are still using hourly billing. It can be tempting, but no client that you want is going to be comfortable with you bad mouthing your competition.

Website

Since most attorneys are still billing by the hour, charging a flat fee is a great way to set yourself apart from other attorneys. I had — what I now can see was far too long — ==an explanation of what value pricing was on my website.== Over time, I whittled it down so that people would actually read it. I think in the beginning I was nervous about what other attorneys, judges, and the bar would think, so I threw everything I could on my website, including the entire section about flat fees from the ABA literature. It was definitely overkill. <u>Don't do this</u>. Your clients want to get a feel for you from your website, so make sure you are professional enough to have a professional website and move on. No one is interested in reading what could be a book, on your actual website.

Fee agreement

Your fee agreement is where you will address any of the ethical issues that could arise out of charging a flat fee. It is imperative that these elements are not only written into your fee agreement, but are highlighted and reviewed with the client so there is no misunderstanding. This is also where you want to pay careful attention to your state's ethical rules in regard to flat fees, as some states mandate particular language in regard to flat fees in fee agreements.

Fee

Obviously, the fee that you are charging is to be written into the fee agreement, front and center.

Conformity with ethical rules

It is important to write that your fee is in conformity with your state's ethical rules for several reasons. The first is that it shows that you have a full understanding of your state's ethical rules. Secondly this language can be important if there is ever a question as the fee itself and whether you can back up whether it is "reasonable".

Earned Upon Receipt and funds will not be placed in trust account

In some states, Earned Upon Receipt is not ethical, so again make sure you are familiar with your RPSs. If that is the case, you will either have to wait until the fee agreement has terminated to move funds from your trust account to your general account, or have certain events or times in the fee agreement for which you have earned X amount of the fee paid. So, you may need to wait a bit to get paid or have a bit more complexity with times or events in which you can pay yourself, but all of the rest of the benefits of using flat fees will remain.

If you are allowed to have Earned Upon Receipt in your state, this language in your fee agreement makes it clear that you have earned and own the funds that have been paid. Also have clear language in your fee agreement that the fees will not be placed in your trust account.

Time limit or event

It is critical that your representation has a time frame or event that will end the representation and that this is clearly spelled out in the fee agreement AND fully discussed with your client. The time frame should be based on the type of case and when things normally conclude in your jurisdiction. The event can be the last step in the proceedings or process of the matter. Use both time and the event in your fee agreement with representation ending upon which occurs first.

For instance, if you are a family law attorney, your representation should cover all events and time that it generally takes to get through at least one mediation or settlement conference. Essentially, representation continues through your first mediation or settlement conference, when it is clear you will be going to trial. In my old jurisdiction, that was generally about five months. So, my fee agreement concluded representation in six months or upon the completion of the first mediation or settlement conference, whichever occurred first. If your jurisdiction takes longer to get through, then extend the time frame.

can we do this in GA?

For estate planning, it was a bit easier as I was mostly in control of when our office got documents done, with a reasonable time frame for the clients to come in and sign them.

So, what time and events make sense for your practice area and your location? When in doubt, push the date out.

What the fee doesn't cover

It is important to put what the fee doesn't cover in your fee agreement. It doesn't cover any work, advice, etc. on any other matter. For instance, in family law, it doesn't cover any other case such as a protection order. In estate planning, it doesn't cover a separate trust.

I also added some "doesn't covers" in family law, such as any representation on an Order to Show Cause in re: contempt. My original fee doesn't cover representation for an accusation of bad behavior on my client's part. Frankly, I never had to use this as my clients kept in line for the most part.

It also does not include any trial preparation or trial, unless that is what you have been hired to do. It is critical to have this language highlighted or you could end up doing a trial for free.

Rules for clients

Your rules for clients will of course differ depending on your practice area. However, they need to be in your fee agreement. For all practice areas, I recommend the following rules in whatever language you want:

- Client will be completely honest with you, including never omitting information.

- Clients will fully cooperate with you and get you requested information or documents by the date requested.

- Client will treat you and your staff with respect at all times.

- Client will not behave in a way in which is likely to harm the case, including but not limited to any criminal behavior or violating any order, in fact or in spirit.

- If flat fee is divided into payments, fees will be automatically charged to card on file. If at any time a payment doesn't go through, you have the right to withdraw from case.

==Make sure that you are reminding clients when any upcoming time or event is taking place, and that the fee agreement will be ending upon that time or event.== I learned this one the hard way. I had a family law client, Laura, who was cooperative, but her husband had the financial data. He was cooperative, but the data was complex with over 32 accounts that we had to sort out. The husband's attorney was also in no hurry to get the case completed. He couldn't be reached. When I did reach him, he would promise to do X and not do it. . . on and on and on. There was absolutely nothing else I could have done to push the case along – God knows I tried. At the end of the time for representation, we had not even set a mediation date. Laura had plenty of funds to continue and paid another fee, but she wasn't really happy about it. She had not truly understood the time frame issue. So, I learned my lesson and not only emphasized the time of representation at the fee agreement discussion, but throughout the case.

I had another case in which my client, Molly, just would not cooperate. We would talk and talk, and she would promise to get me what I needed but she never followed through. I spent more time trying to get her to cooperate than working on her actual matter. I kept telling her that the clock was ticking and that she would not have me as an attorney in X months. I also reminded her that she would not get her money back and I continued to work on the case and counsel her. I even offered to put everything on hold for six months in order to give her more time to move forward. She refused every suggestion and yet still wouldn't fully cooperate. She had paid a small fee and I had spent sufficient time and energy on the matter, including strategic advice, that I had earned my fee. The month coming up to the deadline I was almost begging her to do what we needed to do. After the deadline, I wrote a CYA letter to her about the end of representation. I even offered additional help if she wanted to proceed at another time. Sure enough, a few months later I get a call that she wants her money back as "I didn't do anything" for her.

I waited a day or so to respond from a calm place. I explained the situation to her again, and again offered to even help her with some pleadings. I had more than earned my fee and she would not be getting a refund. Molly actually called me a few days later and apologized. It was a turning point for her to really recognize a very long-standing pattern of hers of burying her head in the sand and not dealing with things she needed to deal with.

Extending your time frame

While I don't recommend having this in your fee agreement, be flexible with your time frames. There are many times when a case is very close to really wrapping up, but the time frame expires. Just finish the case. Clearly this decision is fact based, but 99 out of 100 times just extend the time frame and get it done. I had one case in which the other attorney was to enter final orders, as per our settlement agreement. For whatever reason, he just wouldn't enter the damn orders. I called, emailed, and wrote for months. Finally, I had to tell my client that I thought we were going to have to file a motion to get the orders entered. In fact, we did have to file a motion, and my client had to pay another fee. I kept that fee ridiculously low. Upon receiving the motion, the opposing counsel entered the orders. Unfortunately, my client had to pay a little more due to his ex-wife's choice of attorney. So be it. However, this case was the exception. In others, we were fairly close to wrapping things up and I would just finish the case without any further payment.

So, ==with clear communication, both you and your client will love flat fees. Without clear communication, one of you is going to feel screwed at some point.== Not every element of your fee system needs to be explained to your client, but what is explained must be simple and easily understood. The client's duties, what they are paying for, and when representation ends should be crystal clear to both you and your client. If not, you are going to create issues that you don't need or want.

* * *

CHAPTER SIX
Essential Elements of Flat Fee Billing

Let's remember we're learning not to over complicate. Here are the ingredients to flat fee billing that will make it work properly. Just like baking a cake, all of the ingredients need to be present or it won't work.

Reasonable and spectacular

As we have discussed, a flat fee must be ethical, and thus "reasonable". What is reasonable is of course up for debate and dependent on the circumstances. I would never suggest charging an unreasonable fee. However, you should charge a fee that is high enough to make you want to do a spectacular job. What fee is going to get your attention, get you excited about taking this matter on and doing your finest work? Work that you can look back on and silently smile to yourself with pride. That is the fee you want to charge. Your fees should be on the higher end, if not the highest in town. They reflect your superior work (you had better be providing superior work) and people actually want and are willing to pay higher fees for superior work. ==Your fees are also how prospective clients judge you.==

Consistency in excellence

Your fees need to be consistent with the experience you are providing your client, not just your work product. Yes, we are all providing an experience for our clients whether we or they are aware of it or not. Have you ever been excited about staying at an amazing hotel and were completely fine with paying an exorbitant fee for the privilege? Why in the world would someone pay $600 + for a hotel room that they were just going to sleep in? The answer: for the experience. For the knowing that one is going to have amazing service. For the comfort that nothing is going to be out of place, every detail will be correct, and that if by chance it is not that it will be immediately remedied.

If you are charging superior prices, then you need to demonstrate that you are committed to excellence at every point of contact with your client and that it is about them, not you. That you have invested in yourself and your firm for the client's benefit. You must be consistent or you look like a sham. It isn't about putting on a show for your clients or wearing the most expensive suit.

So yes, your website content matters. You are asking your client to invest a lot with you. Did you invest in quality and excellence, or did you use stock photographs and your web site hasn't been updated in five years? How about your office? When was the last time it was organized, thoroughly cleaned or updated? People do judge you on these things, even if they don't realize it. Why would I assume you are up to date on the law when clearly you haven't updated your décor since 1988? Is your office about you or your client? I have seen so many attorney offices that look like a shrine to themselves. No, you are not impressing anyone. You are demonstrating that you have an enormous ego, are probably insecure, and are more concerned with yourself than your client.

==If you are going to charge excellent fees, you need to be providing excellence at every single client contact, not just in your work product.== That means prompt return of emails or calls, clear communication, clear expectations, always doing what you say you are going to do by when you say you will do it, having a courteous and knowledgeable staff, providing excellent service, and yes, an amazing work product.

==Think about every single point of contact a client or potential client would have with you, your firm, or your work.== How can that point of contact be improved? Is it consistent with the image you want? Does it put the client first? Is it clean or sloppy? If you don't know, ask someone else who is going to be honest with you.

Ability to judge the client, case, and matter in order to set the reasonable fee

For transactional matters, you should have a set fee for each matter. These fees are really not divergent from client to client, unless their matter is different or the value to the client is different. For instance, writing a contract that will involve $20,000 is different than writing a contract involving $2,000,000, and should be charged accordingly.

For Estate Planning, I had set rates that varied dependent on what my client needed and if it were an individual client or married couple. If they needed a trust, what sort of trust, and if our office was funding the trust or not played a part in determining the fee. I also had a separate set of fees for Estates over a certain amount. If I am going to save you $300,000 rather than $30,000, yes, you are going to pay me for that difference as there are different factors involved and higher risk.

For litigation however, you will need to be able to hone in on your ability to judge the client, the case, and overall matter in order to set the fee. This judgment is going to take time, reflection, and some gut checks to develop. Even if you are an inexperienced attorney, listen to your gut. ==Don't ever take on a case because you need the money== when your gut tells you no. Or else charge enough that it makes it worth it knowing the Hell that will befall you.

My second case when I opened my own practice on paper was great. However, even in the initial appointment my client, who I will call Sue, was making statements that were problematic, and I knew they were problematic. She was a victim of domestic violence and very much had a victim mentality. She was highly resistant to my suggestions, very much defending her husband, and didn't "want anything." For those of you who are family law attorneys, I am sure you can sympathize and know where this story is going.

Even looking back on this case nearly 19 years later, I can honestly say I did a great job for Sue. After yet another violent incident involving her husband, and her refusing to take my advice on simple safety issues, I ended up withdrawing from the case. Before doing so, I confirmed my gut feeling with a very wise and experienced attorney. She told me what I knew all along. It was best for me to withdraw. I look back now and I am proud of myself that even then I knew something was wrong and got out when it was evident that there was nothing I was going to do to help Sue.

So even if you don't have years of experience, listen to your gut. Is your client open to listening to you and following your advice? What kind of reputation does the opposing counsel have? Are they going to work to solve problems or throw gas on the fire? If the case looks simple, what are some of the things that could come up that would blow it up? If it involves litigation, who is your judge/court commissioner? What are the social norms in your jurisdiction? I have practiced in rural areas and in Seattle, WA. Each had VERY different social norms. You need to know that fact before going in.

Be humble enough to examine if your fees are appropriate and shift them if they're not

When you first start out, much of setting the fee is going to be a guess. That is fine. Just be humble enough to be able to be honest with yourself if you set that fee too high. Remember, you can always shift them up or down with the next case. I would also note that most attorneys set their fees too low, so keep that in mind.

Ending representation upon a certain event or time

It is imperative that your representation ends, first in time, of either an event or a time frame. Without it, you are arguably on the hook indefinitely. Both the event and the time will depend completely on the matter and circumstances. Again, for instance, for my Estate planning, the event was upon execution of the documents. When my clients signed the final documents, got the originals, copies, etc., my representation ended. That is unless we were funding a trust and then it ended upon the completion of funding. However, it also ended upon a certain date. This date was always far enough out to complete the matter with some cushion. This is important since whether the matter is completed or not is largely out of your control. You don't want to be on the hook indefinitely if a client doesn't cooperate or get you what you need to do your job.

As it stands right now, I have a client, Jayne, who is well past, like over six months past, our time deadline to get us documents in order to fund her trust. We have written and written and only when I informed her that we would be ending representation in two weeks did she send us the documents we need to complete her matter.

It is imperative that you have both triggers of time and an event to end representation and that they be thoroughly understood by your clients.

Having escape clauses

Depending on the matter and jurisdiction, it will be easier to get out of a case in some situations than others. You may need to seek court permission to get out of a case. This can be tricky when you have been paid a flat fee.

You have just as much right, as an attorney being paid hourly, to ethically get out of a case. However, you must have the reasons for getting out of a case in your fee agreement and discuss them with your client.

Crystal clear communication with the client about their responsibilities and the agreement

Not only should your fee agreement contain plain language about what your client's responsibilities are and when representation will end, but you also need to go over this information with them as well. This is more vital in some matters and clients than others. If you have worked with a client previously, they are fairly sophisticated, or it is a transactional matter, you may just need to touch on them briefly.

In a difficult litigation matter though, such as family law or criminal law, then you need to really go over them and be clear that you will get out if their responsibilities are not met. This can be awkward, but it is vital to do. They need to understand that this is not just a CYA provision in your fee agreement. That you will actually get out if they lie to you, lie to the court, sabotage their case, commit a crime, etc.

Being highly efficient

Whether you have more free time or make more money or even as much money as you did with hourly billing will be dependent on you using your time wisely. You need to be efficient. This is so important that I have dedicated an entire chapter on the subject. Absent a strategic reason, you should get the matter concluded promptly. Why in the world have a matter open, sitting on your desk staring at you, any longer than necessary?

Get your work done. Don't procrastinate and get the most out of charging flat fees.

The tips and procedures that you will learn about in Chapter Eight will help even the most seasoned attorney improve their efficiency more than they thought possible.

Keeping sufficient funds in reserve if representation ends early or you need to return funds

There are going to be those rare cases, and I do mean rare, when you will need to give a client money back. You will need to have sufficient reserves in savings in order to be able to do that. For instance, if a client hires you and two days later fires you. Well I can't see a factual situation in which you would have ethically earned your entire flat fee. Therefore, you will need to give some of the funds back, depending on what work you have performed. I speak more on this topic in the next chapter. For now, just know that you are going to need to have a bit of a cushion.

Being a decent human being

Do a great job and earn what you were just paid. Provide actual value to your clients.

Of course you have an ethical duty to provide diligent representation. Using flat fees isn't going to work if you are an unethical or lazy attorney. The whole point is that things are simple, that you go in and get the job done, and do it well. That you are providing value to your clients and being paid for the same.

Unfortunately, I have seen too many — okay one is too many — attorneys who we all just shake our heads at in shame. They are the attorneys who don't communicate with their clients, meet their clients for the first time in court, show up late or not at all to court, postpone hearings time and time again for no valid reason, and are just lazy.

Your client trusted you. Trusted you enough to give you half or the entire fee up front. Yes, you have an ethical and moral duty to get in there and get the job done.

Do not ever abuse this system by not giving it your absolute best because you already have been paid.

The list of necessary ingredients is not terribly long or complex. Keep it simple, and don't overcomplicate it by adding other ingredients to the recipe.

* * *

CHAPTER SEVEN
Essential Elements of Flat Fee Billing

"I have not failed. I just found 10,000 ways that won't work."

Thomas Edison

Attorneys don't tolerate mistakes well. Well, as with anything new in life, there will be issues to address and problems to overcome. That is just part of the learning curve, friend. So here are some of the issues that come up when using flat fees and solutions that I used. These are not the only solutions but they worked well for me. Feel free to try other remedies to see what fits best with you and your practice.

Sticker shock

When I first began using flat fees, I thought that people would freak out at the large number. Much to my delight, it is rare that a client had sticker shock at the price. On those occasions when you do get the shocked look, don't immediately start to defend your price. Many people just need that number to sink in a bit. If a potential client is really having an issue with the price and doesn't understand it, then feel free to briefly explain that ultimately, they would be paying the same or more, but this way they know the price and there are no surprises. Some will come back with their opinion that this is really "a simple matter." I then explain that I do hope so and that if it truly is as simple as they say, that I will have the discretion to adjust the fee downward. BUT, that in my 20 years, as an attorney, this has happened only once. Be clear on the fact that it would take something extraordinary to lower the fee, and that is completely in your discretion.

By and large though, sticker shock has not been the issue that I thought it would be.

Client can't pay the entire fee in one payment

For Estate planning, my clients have a choice. They can either pay the entire fee upfront, which most do, or they can pay half upon hiring me and half when their documents are completed by me. Notice I didn't say when they sign the documents. You can't have your payment dependent on your client. If you have done the work, you need to be paid.

For other matters in which your client needs to break up the payment — that is fine. I would be hesitant to make it a monthly fee as that defeats some of the purpose of using the flat fee. However, two, even three payments, over time is fine. They should be scheduled towards the beginning of the case so that you are assured payment for work completed. I would also make sure those payments are automatic through a credit card or debit card, and give a few days reminder notice of the payment. Again, you don't want to be chasing a client for payment. It should be automatic.

Opposing counsel or judge question fee

While clients don't question the fee generally, opposing counsel or a judge may. There are the unscrupulous, or ill-informed, opposing counsel who upon learning you charged $25,000 love to shout about your outrageous fees. Of course, they only do this at the beginning of the case when their fees are $6,000, but climbing quickly every day. Towards the end of the case, their fees have met or exceeded yours, and they are no longer outraged. Don't let opposing counsel intimidate you or bully you about your fees. You know that your fee is not only reasonable, but a far better value to your client. And you have the data to back up your fees.

I have only had one incident in which a judge questioned my fee. I was in a rural county, in which I had never practiced, arguing a motion for spousal maintenance. The opposing counsel, Cruella, was a local, was not nice, arrived at court more than 30 minutes late, and wasn't bothered about it. She was arguing that my client clearly didn't need spousal maintenance when she had paid my outrageous fee. When Cruella said my fee out loud, there was an audible gasp in the courtroom. This threw me a bit, but once I briefly explained the terms, how they fit in with the ABA guidelines, and how my client had not paid a dime for all of the additional work I had to perform due to Cruella not producing discovery and thwarting settlement discussions, the judge was completely fine with my fees. We did manage to settle the case and of course my fees were actually a tiny bit lower than Cruella's, but my client was far happier than her ex-spouse in regard to their respective attorneys.

Client fires you or you want or need to fire client

Hopefully this situation is rare, but it does happen for a variety of reasons. What to do with the fee and what portion, if any, is to be refunded to your client is extremely fact specific. For both scenarios, it will depend on when the client fires you or you fire the client, what work was performed, the reason your client wants to fire you or vice versa, and what work remains to be completed. These are the main four considerations, although I am sure there are many others that could apply to your specific situation.

If you just began representation and have only performed a bit of work, then it is likely not reasonable to keep the entirety or majority of the fee. Of course, I can see exceptions to this as well. Perhaps the opposing side is intimidated by you and immediately settles for extremely favorable terms for your client. That is incredibly valuable to your client.

Or perhaps it only took you a few hours to find the key piece of evidence that would turn the entire case. That is very valuable to the client, to say the least. Yes, if you just saved your client millions, then you have arguably earned your fee, regardless of how much time you spent on the case or where you are in litigation.

I could go on and on with different factual scenarios. Each case is going to be different. When faced with it, do your due diligence, review the ethics rules, and evaluate whether your client should get a refund, regardless of what your fee agreement says. Do the right thing and if that means giving them money back, then do so.

I had a client, Dan, who hired me for a dissolution of marriage action. It involved a bit of legal research as there were some unusual legal issues in the case. Dan was aware that his case was a mess. Therefore, drafting initial pleadings took a bit longer than it normally would take, and they were not your standard pleadings. They included motions with extensive legal briefing. We had an appointment for him to come in and sign the initial pleadings. When he came in, he brought a friend who not so kindly informed me that I had taken too long to draft pleadings. Dan then fired me.

He then hired a friend of mine who contacted me, and I was able to simply email my friend all of Dan's initial pleadings so that they didn't need to be regenerated. I examined what work had been done and what remained and based on that, I refunded Dan about 75% of the fees he had paid me.

There are also unscrupulous clients, as we all know. There are those clients who once they get a ruling, especially if unfavorable, "want their money back." Fortunately, this is rare. If you have done the work or can otherwise honestly justify your fee, then my advice is to hold your ground, again depending on the circumstances. I am not at attorney who believes that one should routinely cave to clients if they threaten a bar complaint. I don't like being blackmailed.

If you need to do so, and you have any decent relationship with opposing counsel, you can always cover yourself by asking them if their fees have met or exceeded X. That way if a bar complaint is filed over fees, and the bar investigates, which is rare over fees, then you have concrete justification for your fees that can't really be argued with.

Also make sure you review your State's RPCs in regard to how to handle any disputed funds.

You miscalculated the fee

If you miscalculated the fee to be extremely too high, and you can't justify keeping the entire fee, then do the right thing and give your client some money back. They will be surprised and thrilled. Talk about creating good will and an amazing reputation for having integrity. This, by the way, has never happened in my practice. But it could.

What about the other way? You misread the case and it blew up. That is on you friend. You are just going to have to suck it up. You still need to do an excellent job for your client. Remember you have a time frame or event, so there is an end date to the representation. You will either stop the hemorrhaging or get more funds at that end date, but for now you just need to suck it up.

This has only happened once to me. I had charged a solid fee, as I knew the case was going to be a mess. However, when the opposing party hired a new attorney, he blew the case out of the water. I just had to do what needed to be done. My representation didn't change a bit.

It is rare for you to see a case blowing up, I hope. At the end of the day, you are making enough money that it really doesn't bother you to work a bit more on one or two cases. So, if there is something for you to learn from the experience about setting fees then fine. If not, just move on and don't worry about it.

Case is closed, but not done, when representation end date arrives

In most cases, I just finish the work. It is not a big deal for me and clients appreciate the effort.

Client disappears

Your client has hired you, paid you, maybe you have done a bit of work, or not, and then your client drops off the face of the earth. While incredibly rare, it has happened to me. Especially with Estate Planning, people can be funny, and they are very resistant to finalizing the process and thus admitting their mortality.

I have not been able to find any specific ethical rule or opinion that deals with this issue.

What I did in this situation is that I completed as much of the work as I possibly could. After I had attempted to contact my client in every way possible, I sent them the drafted documents. While the documents were not signed by them, they could sign them at any time, with a notary and witnesses. I can't force someone to come into my office to sign their Estate Planning documents. These clients can contact me at any time, and we can finish off the process. If they contacted me years from now, we would need to examine whether they needed to pay additional fees, as the documents would probably need to be revised.

If on the other hand you haven't done any of the work then after a sufficient time and letters to your client, return any appropriate fees.

Your client is seeking attorney fees from opposing party

If your client is seeking attorney fees, then you are going to need to do a bit of educating the court on flat fees and most likely use an hourly rate and time in your argument for asking for X amount in attorney fees. "If I were to charge by the hour, my hourly fee would be X and I would have spent Y time on the matter in question, so I am seeking Z." If it is a reasonable request, then you using flat fees shouldn't be an issue or have any bearing on whether you do or do not get fees awarded.

When you change to flat fees, issues will come up, but they are relatively easy to address — especially if you do what you should do as your guide rather than just what you have a right to do. Some of these issues you can learn from and others you just need to move on from. Just remember this is how we learn. It isn't a bad thing.

* * *

CHAPTER EIGHT
Time Management Tools of Successful Attorneys

"Time is far more valuable than money. You can get money back, never time."

Jim Rohn

Most attorneys I know feel that they are not in control of their time. They must drop everything when that new motion lands on their desk. That one phone call can change their entire day's plans. A good client says, "I need it now," and we switch our entire week's work plans. While this profession, and the various practice areas within it, are less amenable to planning one's time, it is possible to remain at the reins rather than constantly feel like you are being dragged behind the horse.

If one wants to take the efficiency of flat fees to the next level and create even more time for one's self, the use of certain tools is necessary. I used to believe that I was fairly good at managing my time. Certainly, better than most other attorneys I knew. However, I took my skills to an entirely different level after I took a course by Darren Hardy on time management. Much of the information below is based on his work.

One task only, please

I know I am going to get flak for this one, but there is no such thing as being able to multitask. I could never multitask and felt like something was wrong with me when others would brag about their ability to multitask. Study after study is now demonstrating that multitasking is simply not possible. Your brain is only able to focus on one thing at a time. So, when you are multitasking, what you are doing is cognitively switching back and forth between activities. You are not completing either cognitive function as you keep switching back and forth.

When you multitask, it is inevitable that each individual task will be slower and of lower quality as you are going back and forth. Ask yourself why you are doing this activity? Is it to just mark it off the list or is it to get some result? Is your goal, in having a conversation with your client, so that you can say you talked to them, or is it to actually listen to what they are saying and know that they have listened to you as well?

You simply cannot have quality while multitasking. As much as you may feel you are being productive, you are not going to be productive if you multitask. When practicing law, every moment is going to count. It is imperative that you have quality results, which will occur if you only perform one task at a time.

Not convinced? Fine. Humor me and try it for one day. Just for one day do one single task at a time. No multitasking. How did it feel? Were you able to do it? Were you able to actually enjoy your lunch today? Did you actually remember the conversation you had with a colleague or your child?

Removing other distractions or interruptions

When you are an attorney, it can feel like you are in a sea of piranhas all nipping at you trying to take a bite. Given the interruptions that we face, it is frankly surprising we can get anything done. Clients call, opposing counsel calls, we have court, client meetings, and staff comes in with questions all day long.

To take your time management to the next level, you must remain in control of your time to the largest extent possible. The first step it to protect it. The most immediate solution, and one that will have an instant effect, is to reduce or eliminate interruptions and distractions. How you do this will of course depend on your work situation. The important thing is that it be done, and you protect that time with your life.

After uni-tasking, I hope that you are convinced that you do a better job if you focus on one task at a time. Here is another incredibly powerful tool to help you keep your focus on the task at hand: eliminate distractions and interruptions. This will be most useful at work so that when we are at work, we are producing at a high level and getting results. Most of us have heard that it takes 10-23 minutes for our brain (or thereabout) to fully regain focus after an interruption or distraction. Yes, you might get back to your task or project, but your brain isn't 100% in yet.

I am not going to go into detail about how many distractions and stimuli we have in our world. I don't have the time. Suffice it to say that all of this new technology that is supposed to make our lives easier, and give us more time, not only hasn't, but it is causing us to be far less productive.

In order to really use any of the tools in this chapter, you are going to have to focus. You can't focus if you are getting alerts for every like, text, or email or even checking to see if you got any likes, texts, or emails.

Step one is to ==cut the cord.== Not entirely, but technology and your smart phone should work for you, not for you to be a slave to an inanimate object. So, when you are driving, put the phone in the back seat. Not kidding. Not only may you save a life, but you can actually relax a bit in the car. Have a real conversation with one of your kids. ==There is nothing you need to do on your phone while you are driving. Really.==

==When you are at home put your phone away.== You are supposed to be with your family. They deserve your undivided attention. Likewise, at work. This doesn't mean put your phone face down. It means turn off notifications and put it out of your line of sight.

There are plenty of distractions we can do nothing about. The dog is going to bark. The kids are going to come running through the house, and your assistant is just going to have to talk to you. However, there are a lot of things we can do to reduce the interruptions and distractions. The largest one is to ==silence your phone.== Turn off notifications on everything. Silence your phone — not even on vibrate. Instruct your family to call your office in the event of an emergency. People were able to contact other people well before smartphones came along.

At the office, close your office door and give strict instructions that no one is to knock or open that door. If there is bone or blood then call 911, but no one interrupts you during the next 90 minutes... or whatever. If you have a big project, and know how difficult it will be to do in peace, go to the library and get a private room to work in. I have known of authors who have rented hotel rooms and taken the phone off the hook so they could write in peace. If the project is at home, hire a sitter to take the kids out for the day, so that you can have the house to yourself and really focus. Even just 90 minutes of real focus will produce results like you cannot imagine.

You control your time. There are plenty of other people out there who will steal it if you let them. Just think of the two scenarios below.

You have a response or other pleading due on Monday and you are going to have to work on it during the weekend. It should only take a few hours.

Old way:

Procrastinate on Saturday, do errands, grocery shop, do laundry, transport kids to activities . . . and use all of that time to not focus on the pleading that you need to draft. You are not focused on your kids even though they are with you. You are still thinking about the pleading. It is haunting you. You are probably not as patient with your kids and don't really engage with them as part of your brain is still thinking about the pleading.

You finally get to it on Sunday afternoon. You are trying to work on it and feeling the pressure as you know you have a limited time to do it. The freaking kids are not cooperating, nor do they care about your client much less this pleading being due. They are still playing, yelling, walking by, and trying to talk to you while your phone rings a few times as well. You are either missing the game you wanted to watch or you have it on, but on mute.

Your drafting is not getting done quickly, and you know it is not great work. Then the next time someone runs through the house or heaven forbid tries to talk to you, what do you do? You snap. "I told you I had work to do!" Now you are upset. Your family is upset. And you still haven't finished drafting the pleading. In your mindset, even if now your family is yelled into being quiet, what do you think your work product is going to be? Not your best.

You finally get it drafted and feel some relief. Now you have to go and try to do damage control with your family.

New way:

Friday evening, schedule your two hours of work time for Saturday morning if possible. Tell your family about it and ask for their help so that you can get this work done. Explain to them how it is difficult to concentrate and focus, so that for two hours you are going to go to the library, office, home office, or wherever to work. Then go separate yourself so that you can do that. Turn off any way for people to reach you. Get your work done.

Given your focus, you will probably be done before the allotted two hours and your work product will be a quality product. Now, you are relaxed and can actually spend time with your family and be present with them on more than just a physical level. No yelling, no regrets, no drama, and no guilt.

You are also teaching others, through example, how to focus and concentrate. Something younger generations are going to have to learn given being raised with tablets, smartphones, and constant stimulation. Maybe they even do their own homework at the same time you are doing yours. Then the whole family can relax all weekend knowing their most important tasks are done.

Prioritize and limit tasks

One is not going to get results, or be productive, without separating vital work from trivial work. This is the difference between being busy and really getting work done and getting results. You are never going to be able to get it all done. There is always something else that you could be doing. What counts and what is going to make the difference is getting the right things done — the important things done.

Once you get the vital things done, you can feel free to let the rest or the tasks go knowing they don't really matter. You can do anything once you stop trying to do everything.

Time blocking

Some of you will have heard about time blocking. It is simply blocking off time on your calendar to do certain tasks. So, for instance you only see clients on certain days and times of the week. You do all of your practice management duties on a set day and times of the week or you meet with your legal assistant about cases every morning from 8:30 – 9:00. The point is that you are adding consistency and dedicating time, ahead of time, to important tasks. Make sure you also have set aside extra time to deal with the unexpected issues that arise every day and week.

Time blocking is a great way of ensuring that no important duties fall through the cracks, gives your staff comfort in that they know that you will be available on certain days and times to go over things, and puts you back in control of your calendar. Of course, this only works if you stick with the schedule. It can be difficult to stick with it, but once you do it religiously for a few months, it will become a habit and I think you will find it works well.

Jam sessions

Ninety-minute jam sessions are related to time blocking. These are sessions in which you put up the do not disturb sign on your door, turn off the phone, and just grind it out for ninety minutes. You will be amazed at how much high-quality work you can get done in ninety minutes of completely focused time.

Ninety minutes is about as long as anyone can focus, much less on a difficult task, before they need a break. I wouldn't try to do more than ninety minutes at a time as you will lose focus and your work product will suffer. So, take a good 15-20-minute break, and if you can, do another 90-minute session.

Each task may not take the full 90 minutes. That is fine. If one task is complete, then go to the next. Your 90-minute session may be all focused on practice management issues. Make a to-do list and focus on them and get them done.

Depending on your practice area, you may be able to even do three sessions a day a few days a week. Even if you are in court frequently, there will still be plenty of time when you are in your office. When you are in the office, schedule your sessions and focus for the full 90 minutes.

Once you try using this tool you will be so pleased with how much you get accomplished, I predict you will continue to use it. This is especially true if you have a large project that realistically is best to tackle a bit at a time. If you can work on it consistently for 90 minutes from three – five times a week, you will get it done easily.

Saying no

Your ability to produce results, and when you are an attorney stay sane, is going to largely also depend on your ability to say "no". I think, especially for women, we have not only not been taught to say "no", but we have been taught it is not nice to say "no". It is imperative to be able to be comfortable saying "no". Otherwise you become a martyr — overtaxed, overwhelmed, burned out, and people will steal your time.

If you don't want to burn out as an attorney, you are going to have to learn to say "no". "No", to new assignments that someone is asking you to do because they are lazy and don't want to do it. "No", to new or even existing bar volunteer or pro bono "opportunities". "No", to that party you don't really want to go to. "No", to baking cupcakes for that event. This isn't going to be easy. We get a lot of pressure from others to participate in pro bono activities that frankly we all know don't help people much. Or bar activities that maybe produce 15 minutes worth of quality work or discussion in the two hours it took to have a meeting, not including the travel time. If you are in a firm, you may not be able to say "no" to much. I get it. However, the more you respect your time and begin to say "no", the more others will begin to respect your time.

When you are in a situation in which you do have free will, then may I suggest you start to employ this lifesaving decision maker. If I can't instantly say "Hell yes" then it is a "no". If I have any hesitation, resistance, or ahhh, then the answer is "no". I don't have time in my life for anything that is not a "Hell yes." Every minute you are spending doing something that is not really important to you, you are taking that time away from what is important to you.

This leads me to your three main priorities.

Three main priorities

During any time in our lives, we should only really focus on three priorities at a time. More than that is just too much. These priorities change over time as life changes; however, all of our tasks should relate to our three priorities. If your number one most important task today is not related to your three main life goals, why is it a priority? This used to be one of my main life issues. I would have all of these goals, but my daily tasks were not related to them or if tasks were on my to do list, I wouldn't make them a priority. For instance, I would say that my health and losing weight were a top priority, and yet even if exercising got on the to do list, I didn't make it a priority and by the time I got to it, it is 7:00 p.m. and there was no way I was going to do it. I had nothing left. All of these other tasks had taken priority over the tasks that would have actually gotten me to the goals that I said were important to me.

Now my tasks are based on what my three main priorities are at any given time. The tasks that are not related to my three priorities either don't get done at all or they are done only when all other tasks have been completed. This tool really helped me be more disciplined and was a weekly and daily reminder of what my real priorities were.

Keeping in mind your three priorities makes decision making easier. When the choice is between getting that pleading completed vs. going to your kid's soccer practice, then the decision is easier as you are reminded that actually participating in your kids' lives is one of your three priorities. Practicing law cannot be your only priority in life. Not if you want any sort of a life.

Weekly planning

Every week, I write out all of the things I need to do, should do, and want to do for the following week. I then use a chart with my three priorities on the chart as well as another category. Each of the items in my to do list must fit into one of the categories. For instance, my current three categories are: health (physical, emotional, spiritual); income & impact (firm and book); and continuing to simplify life as much as possible. These categories are what matter in my life now. As I was writing my first book, my father's health declined, and he died. I had to shift my priorities a bit to give myself time to heal and rest. I also had to add handling his services and estate.

If one of your "to do's" doesn't fit into one of your three categories, it goes into the "other" category. I then really examine the "other" list. What can I hire someone else to take care of on the list? What can I delegate to my assistant to take care of for me? What can I just eliminate as it is not a "Hell yes"? Obviously, some things you just need to do yourself, such as going to the dentist.

I then go back to the three categories and start calendaring. It is important, actually vital, to calendar your tasks or else your calendar and day will fill up with items that are not priorities and not furthering your three main goals.

If having a better relationship or connection with your spouse or kids is one of your goals, then it needs to be on the list. You need to have actual things to do each week to reach that goal. You are going to need to spend some time and energy to make those connections. So, write in talking X number of hours to your spouse, spending X hours one on one with your child where you are connecting, or reading a book this week on relationships.

So, my daily calendar is planned out so that I get what is important to my goals done every day. Then if I have extra time, which I generally do as I haven't been wasting it, then I can get to some of the "to do's" in the "other" category.

On your daily to do list or calendar, do the hardest thing first. It isn't going to go away. It will haunt you the entire day. Just bite the bullet and get it done. Then the rest of the day is easy by comparison. We all know this right? We all have had those tasks that we kept putting off as we don't want to do them. But then they just haunt us all day. Just do it and get it over with.

Now keep in mind that when practicing law, your entire day's plan or week's plan can go up in smoke at any moment. Know that ahead of time and be okay with that reality. Hopefully with this plan, you will have your most important tasks completed.

Outsourcing

I used to have such a problem with the idea of hiring someone to help me do something I could do myself, especially when money was tight. I can do a lot of things myself. I knew my time should be valuable, but until I did the math, I really didn't understand or compute just how much.

What I didn't understand was that my time was worth a lot even in the hours that I wasn't "earning" money. My "time off" was best used to do what I needed to do in order to refresh, revive, and enjoy life, so I could be fully ready to work and work well the next day. Every minute of every day was valuable.

I know many solo practitioners who say you don't have the money to hire people. You might need to work harder to earn that extra few hundred dollars a month to pay for that housekeeper and then that will free up more time to make more money.

You say you're not comfortable with other people doing for you. Well, you can stay in your comfort zone or you can be a bit uncomfortable for a little bit and have more time and more money. Here are your two choices. You can either accept some help, get more done, and have a bit of peace or you can continue on with how things are going.

Learn from my mistakes. When I started my own practice, I did my own bookkeeping for years. That is even though I received poor grades in accounting in college and hated every minute of bookkeeping. When I finally hired a bookkeeper, I felt instant relief. It was not terribly expensive either.

It has never been easier to hire people to do specific tasks that can really help your firm. Perhaps you don't need to hire a full-time staff person. You can outsource all of your marketing tasks, bookkeeping, drafting tasks, or other tasks that are not a good use of your time.

So, what are some things that you could get some help with right now?

Ego

I am sure you don't, but many other attorneys have large egos — to state the obvious. How much time do we waste, and how many problems do we cause for our clients because of our ego? The answer is ugly if we are honest with ourselves. We waste a lot of time and cause many issues for ourselves and our clients because we let our ego get the better of us. Yeah, I am as guilty as the rest of you.

As difficult as it is to take a few minutes to calm oneself and set your ego aside, the following tools — when I am self-aware enough to use them — help.

Set phone appointments instead of email

It is far more productive to have a phone conversation with a client or opposing counsel then it is to go back and forth with email. Just picking up the phone and calling opposing counsel is not productive because most of the time he or she is not available and even if they were, they are not prepared to talk with you in a productive manner as they are doing something else.

I have found it very productive to call and set an appointment with opposing counsel to discuss whatever issue you are having in the case. That way you are not playing phone tag and not going back and forth in emails (where tone is difficult to decipher.) Opposing counsel should be prepared to talk about the case and have answers, and you are having a conversation that will actually produce some results. Certainly, you'll get more results than any email exchange. This is especially true when needing to discuss a hot or difficult issue.

People are also far more pleasant in person or on the phone than in email. The people who have no problem sending emails that are on fire, are generally much more pleasant when you actually speak with them.

I know we have been taught to cover our ass and get it in writing. On one or two cases, I have even had to submit email exchanges to the court. Do you really think a judge wants to read the email exchange you had with the opposing counsel? No, they do not.

If you feel the need to document the conversation, then go ahead and write an email to the opposing counsel. After the conversation, indicate your understanding of whatever and that if your understanding is not correct, then to please let you know.

Done is better than perfect

Many of us are perfectionists. We don't tolerate being incorrect. We don't tolerate it with ourselves and we don't tolerate it with each other and can be rather horrid to both. Yes, it is important to write so that it is easy to understand, conveys the correct and important facts, and has all of the other vital ingredients to persuade. Sloppy is not acceptable. Inaccurate is not acceptable. However, perfect shouldn't be our standard. Going for 100% in everything we do is not doing our clients any favors and not good for us either.

I remember my writing professor emphasizing how if your work could be better, you weren't done. I completely disagree. A perfectly worded motion is not going to be the deciding factor in a dispute. Yes, a poorly worded one can be a distraction and all of the necessary information must be contained, but no dispute has been won or lost because the pleadings haven't been perfectly edited or the oral argument was not memorable.

Our clients are not paying us for a perfectly written pleading or the most eloquent oral argument. They are paying us for our judgment, to know what facts are or are not important, to know what is in their best interest, and to be able to articulate the same. They are paying us to get results or at least give it a good faith effort to get results.

So do a great job, do your best, and then stop. Done is better than perfect. And by all means remember that shorter is better than longer.

If you use some of the tools above, you will multiply the time you are saving using flat fees. You will instantly set yourself apart from other attorneys.

As attorneys, most of the time, we are highly reactive, running incredibly quickly and not making the impact that we would like. We're not being as productive as we would like or think we really should be. So, we keep running faster, adding more and more hours to our workday, and still don't get the really important things done. Those important tasks also include effort and time with our family and ourselves.

Imagine a world in which you could be an amazing attorney; bring in as much or more than you or your competitors are, and work less than 40 hours a week. Yes, this dream is possible. How do I know? I did it and so can you.

Using flat fees is a powerful tool and when multiplied by amazing time management tools, your productivity will skyrocket. You will be doing superior work in far less time.

* * *

CHAPTER NINE
Is This Working?

"Those who say it can't be done shouldn't interrupt those doing it."

Chinese proverb

When I first began writing and speaking about flat fees someone would comment that X element wasn't ethical. At first I would be concerned that I had missed something, would instantly do more research and after one comment even called the bar association's ethics hotline. In each case the accusations about something being unethical were flat out wrong. And not by a little bit. Again, when you are doing something that is novel people are going to be nervous, and some will be nasty. Don't let that intimidate you. You have done your own research, know your RPSs, and are doing things properly.

It takes courage to go against tradition and do something differently. Especially in a culture that worships tradition and the status quo. However, the results of flat fees speak for themselves, but only if you recognize them.

So, I would suggest that you take a bit of time after you start using flat fees to reflect and see what is working and what may need to be tweaked. Perhaps look at your fee structure in six months, and then again after a year.

It is easy to not recognize whether something is working or not if you don't look at it and measure it. So, ask yourself what are you getting accomplished now? Is it more than when you used hourly fees? How much more time do you have now? Would you ever go back to hourly fees? If you are using flat fees properly, then frankly you should have no temptation to ever go back to using hourly fees.

What is the bottom line? Is your life simpler with flat fees? Are you more content in your practice? What does success in regard to flat fees look like? I don't know. That is for you to decide. However, I would argue that even if all you have done is removed the annoyance of having to do time sheets every day … that is a success. My guess is that you have accomplished far more.

A word of caution though. When you have extra time, if you don't intentionally fill it, life will. What I mean by that is if you have extra time you don't know what to do with, you will be tempted to fill it with busy work that is not productive and same cycle you just worked to get out of. So, think about how you want to fill your time. What will you do with the extra time each week? Make that a priority so that you don't find yourself filling your days with nonsense.

Additionally, the more you share your experiences using flat fees, the more you will help other attorneys and our profession. I believe that self examination is a good thing, even though it can be uncomfortable. So have the courage to speak up about your experience and share any hints or issues that you discover on your journey.

* * *

CONCLUSION

"What we fear of doing most is
usually what we most need to do."

Ralph Waldo Emerson.

Using flat fees properly will significantly improve your satisfaction with practicing law, increase your time outside of your practice without losing income, and perhaps even increase your income.

What do you have to lose by trying flat fees? Absolutely nothing, assuming of course it is ethical for your practice area in your state. Heck if I can do it successfully in family law litigation, then any practice area can do it.

"Someday" is not a day of the week. So, pick a date to begin to implement and a due date to start with your first client. Try it for at least six months. Then evaluate how your office, bank account, and life feel about flat fees. If you don't like it, you can always go back. However, I doubt you will as the reality is amazing. Just think of the possibilities.

Imagine what your life will be when you get back hundreds of hours a year by not having to deal with the administration associated with hourly rates alone. Imagine the reduced anxiety of not having to worry about who will pay, when, and how much. Imagine your firm's morale when there are not any billable hourly requirements. Imagine being an attorney creating a great work product, having your clients value that work, and paying an amazing price for it. Imagine not wasting a single moment of any day.

This is not a fairy tale. It could be your life.

* * *

ABOUT BRITA LONG

Brita Long is an AV-rated Estate Planning Attorney, Writer, and Speaker. She is licensed in Washington State and Texas and has practiced law since 1997. She has been a mother, step mother, daughter, sister, wife, ex-wife, business owner, amateur trapeze artist, and has wing walked over the Salish Sea. She has saved two old homes from certain death. She lives in Austin, Texas with her dog Bear.

You can learn more about her or work with her at: britalong.com

Made in the USA
Columbia, SC
18 January 2020